The Jackson County Library Foundation gratefully acknowledges
the Ben B. Cheney Foundation
for its generous grant to expand the library collection.

BEN B. CHENEY FOUNDATION
Helping people and their communities

Jackson County Library Foundation 541-772-4601 www.jclf.org

GLORIOUS
PAPERS

G L O R I O U S
P A P E R S

R U T H   I S S E T T

B T BATSFORD • LONDON

Text and designs
© Ruth Issett 2001

The moral right of the author
has been asserted.

Photographs © B T Batsford Ltd
2001

Published in 2001 by
B T Batsford
64 Brewery Road
London N7 9NT

A member of **Chrysalis** Books plc

Reprinted 2003

A catalogue record for this book is available from
the British Library.

ISNB 0 7134 8669 4

Printed in Spain
Photography by Michael Wicks

Distributed in the United States and Canada by Sterling Publishing Co.,
387 Park Avenue South, New York NY 10016, USA

RUTH ISSETT lives in Kent with her family, who continue to be amazed that she
manages a balancing act between co-ordinating Adult Education courses,
teaching embroidery, textile and design courses both nationally and
internationally, as well as working on her own colour-related projects in both
paper and fibre – and writing the occasional book.

ACKNOWLEDGEMENTS
I would like to thank other tutors and students who have inspired me to write
this book. To Viv and Kevin who encourage me to demonstrate techniques, to
Barbara and Jill for their dependability and friendship. To Lucy, Olly, Adam, Ali and
Chas for keeping me on track, as well as all their encouragement and continued
interest in all my mad projects.

CONTENTS

Introduction

This book has one main purpose – to encourage you to start colouring and making glorious papers and then to use them in any way you might find appropriate. From the moment you view and then handle some of the huge range of papers available, your fingers will itch to start working with them and your eyes will focus on wonderful combinations. Just arranging differently coloured sheets, laying out assorted textures, or feeling individual types of fibre, is sufficient to bring the senses under assault.

The addition of a rich inky stream of pure colour to a paper surface can stimulate a torrent of excited emotions. The paper immediately changes, revealing hidden fibres and qualities, and the results cannot be predicted.

This is the challenge of glorious papers: the combinations of paper, ink, paint and other media are so varied and infinite that no two papers need ever be the same. There may be similarities, but the next addition of colour or glaze or varnish can totally alter the effect.

This book shows how to use papers to develop design ideas and employ decorated surfaces as a key that will unlock your imagination, develop your skills, and give you the chance to practise your colour mixing. More than anything else, these papers offer a chance to enjoy the process of being creative, so allow yourself time to play, to handle all the papers, to be absorbed in the processes, and to observe what happens when one colour meets another or one surface is laid against another.

Before you start to use the techniques described here, try to make time to read the book, as well as look at the pictures, and then please have a go. Lay down the newspaper, and place a large sheet of white paper on top. Get out all the art materials, equipment and papers you are going to use. Lay the white paper on top of the newspaper, not just to protect the table underneath, but to experiment with dabs of your colours, or as the over-spill area for your painting. I have often found that I love that piece of paper, and that even the newspaper that is under everything often looks wonderful at the end of a working session!

Illustration: Pearl Ex coloured iridescent lustre powders.

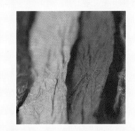

one

Papers, Materials and Equipment

In recent years, the range of papers and dyes available to artists and craftspeople has expanded at an amazing – and exciting – pace. The following section lists the different materials and equipment used to create the delicious illustrations that follow.

Illustration: Unusual papers: papyrus (top); kozo bamboo plait (centre); kozo bamboo stripe (bottom).

UNDERSTANDING YOUR MATERIALS

(Preceding page)
Coloured Indian cotton
rag papers.

If you are to achieve similar – and hopefully better – results, it is important to understand the materials and equipment that you will use. Treat this section as a starting point or a reference document. The most important thing is to get out the inks, acrylics, bronze powders, papers and paint brushes that you have been hoarding and start to use them.

As you try different techniques be aware of the following points.

- Is the colour adhering to and affecting the paper?
- Is the paper absorbing or resisting the colour?
- How does one paper differ from another?
- How do the different media respond to each other?
- How experienced are you at using these techniques, materials and equipment?
- Are you aware of your own skills?
- Are you in a hurry, or are you very absorbed?
- Are you 'clumsy' when you paint, or are you very sensitive to the type and surface of the paper?
- Are you very logical and methodical as you work, or is your work area a sea of discarded papers, brushes and materials?

▶▶ Coloured mulberry
tissue silk and
banana paper.

There is no right or wrong way to create glorious papers, but you do need to be sensitive. Be aware of how and why effects are achieved, and be able to evaluate the results.

PAPERS

In addition to the standard papers used by the general public, such as brown wrapping paper and cartridge, an ever-increasing range of handmade papers is available to artists and designers. Some of the handmade papers are sized (coated with a protective surface), while others are very absorbent.

A great variety of coloured papers is now produced commercially, including exotic metallic papers, such as Keaykolour and Hispeed papers. Be aware, however, that ready-coloured papers, such as those produced for children, may be made from recycled pulp. These types are consequently very absorbent and may be unsuitable for use with dyed and inked techniques, producing muddy results.

Handmade papers are made from a wide range of fibres, including banana, mulberry, silk, straw, cotton, and kozo plant, and are available in a variety of weights and finishes. There are fine tissues, such as Japanese Sanwa, Gampi, or Nepalese lokta and mulberry, as well as banana papers. These are as fine as a delicate fabric, and colour with ink and dyes beautifully.

Heavily textured papers include lokta huck and wood dust, or rough banana and Indian ruched paper, which is like a seersucker fabric. The soft, absorbent kozo papers often have other materials, such as bamboo strip and fibres, imbedded into the surface.

Many of these papers are very strong, being made from long fibres, and can therefore be used for design as well as collage, sewing and all types of decorative techniques.

▶ Range of
Keaycolour and
commercial papers.

(Overleaf) Straw silk
Fontana paper,
Japanese Sanwa paper,
and mulberry tissue
silk.

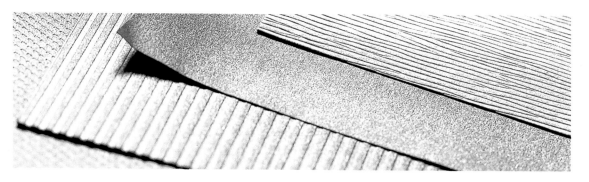

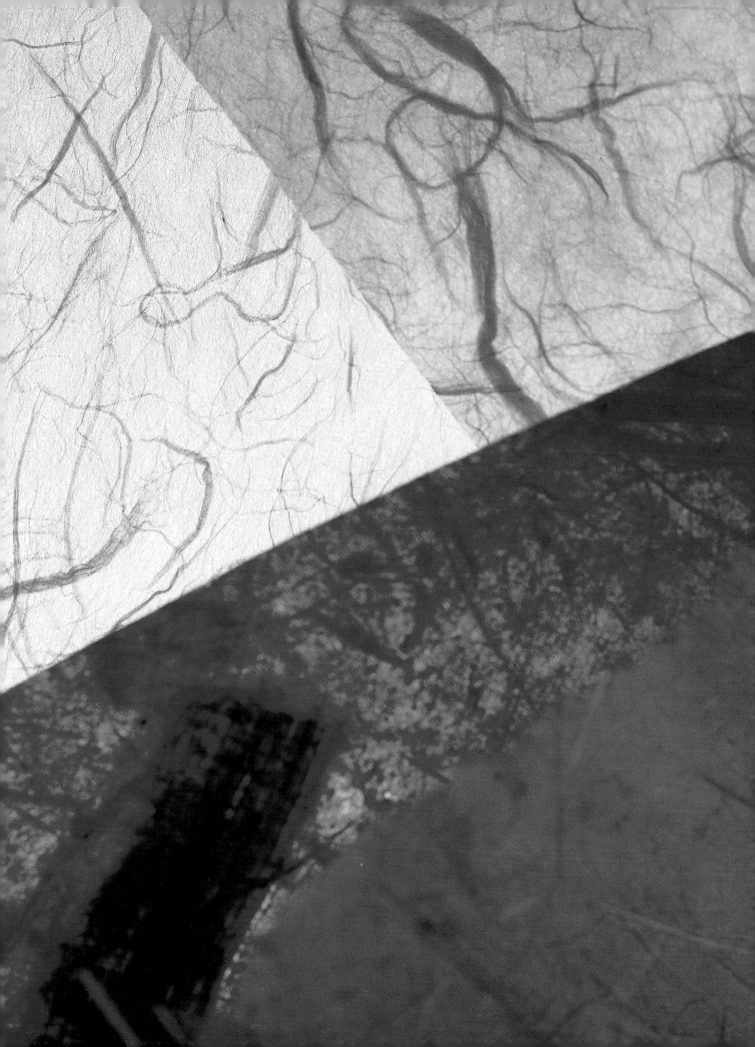

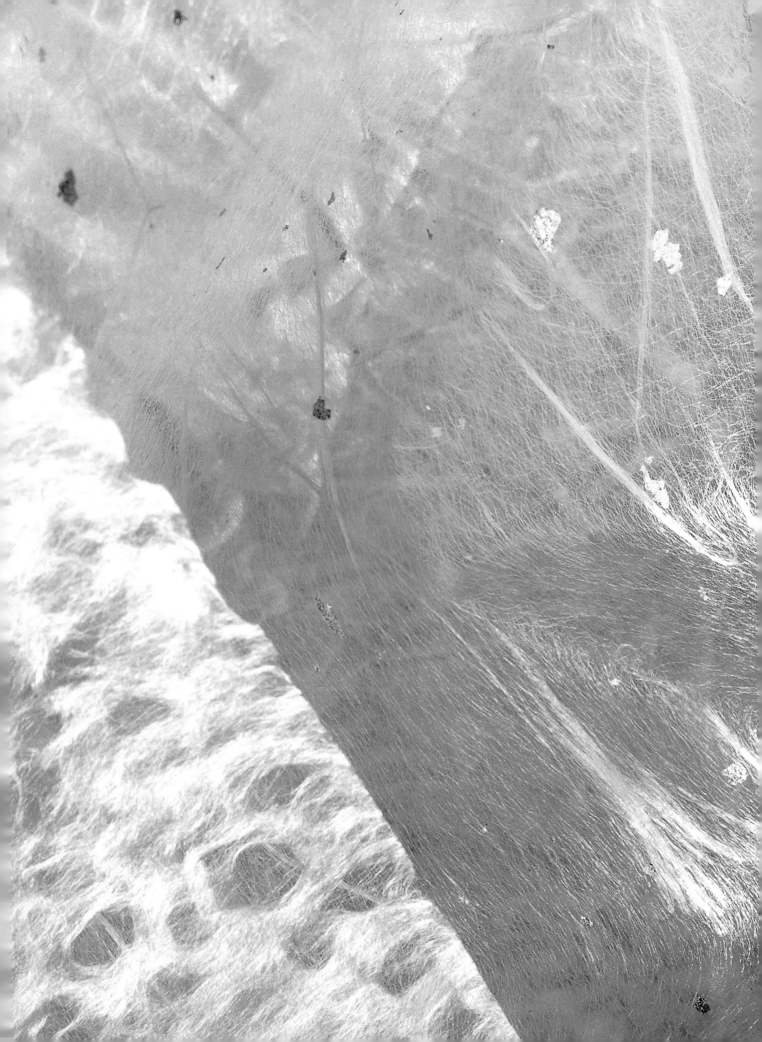

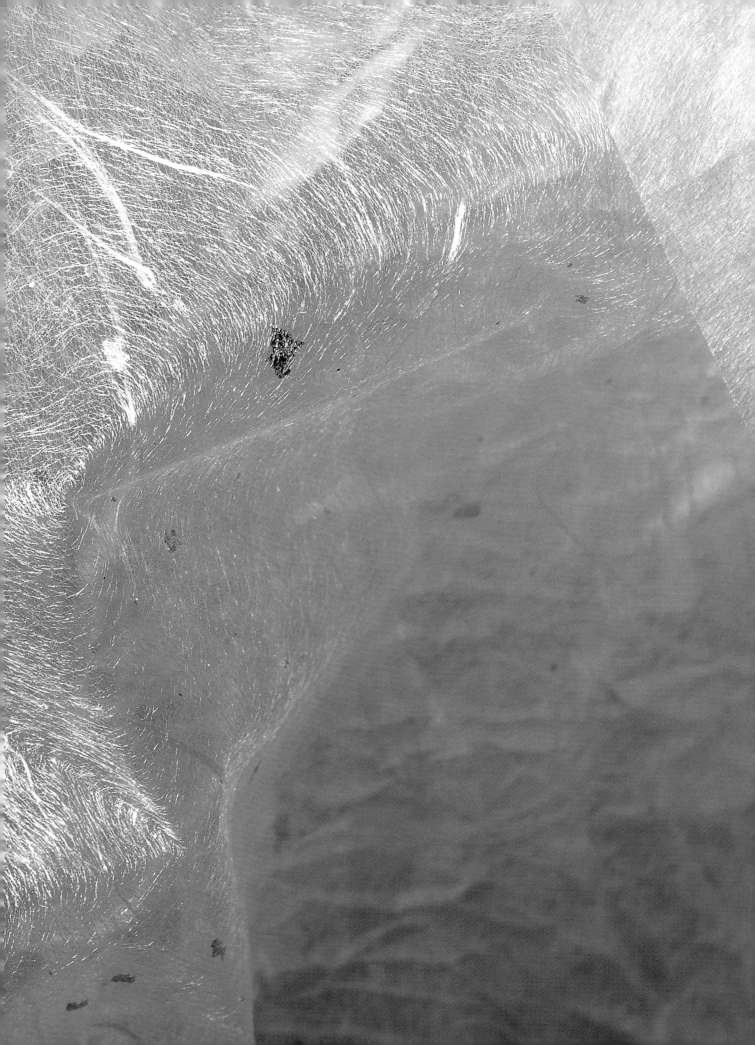

(Preceding page)
Indian cotton rag
papers plus lokta
walnut, lokta wood
dust, and lokta huck.

▼ Selection of
handmade Indian, Thai,
and Japanese papers.

- **Brown** Plain brown wrapping paper, available in a large number of textures ranging from almost translucent to thick and sturdy types, has its uses. While the brown base colour will affect the final result, the paper can be used to good effect with various colouring media.
- **Cartridge** This is also available in several weights, and is usually white or cream in colour.
- **Indian rag papers** Handmade, using long-fibred cotton rags, this paper has surface sizing and deckle edges.
- **Southern Indian rag papers** These are made from cotton rags textured with tropical plant fibres: bagasse (with sugar-cane fibre), banana (with banana leaf fibres), gunny (with jute fibre), straw and tea. Another version has fine wool fibres embedded in the surface, producing a mottled effect.
- **Indian silk** Long silk fibres are laid on the surface of a soft cotton paper.
- **Lokta** This translucent paper is made from the bark of the lokta plant. A strong paper, it wrinkles when inked. Lokta ranges in colour from cream to brown.
- **Mulberry tissue** A lightweight tissue made from the bark of the mulberry tree.
- **Tissue** Commercial tissue papers are widely available. Lightweight, smooth and delicate, they can be fragile, especially when wet, but are useful for layering. Tissue paper becomes transparent when varnished.

COLOURING MEDIA

In addition to the colouring agents described below, a wide range of oil and wax artist's materials, such as oil pastels, wax crayons and wax candles, as well as specialist Sennelier iridescent oil pastels, can be used successfully with inks to produce exciting effects on paper.

- **Procion dyes** These fibre-reactive powdered dyes are designed for dyeing natural fibres in cold water. However, a small quantity – half a teaspoon – of dye powder, mixed with about 50 ml (3 tbsp) of warm water, produces a wonderfully strong water-based ink that is excellent for applying to all types of paper. Dyes vary in strength, however: lemon yellow and golden yellow require double the usual quantity of dye powder, for example, whereas magenta will require less powder. The dyes can be mixed to ink, labelled, and stored in airtight jars for a number of weeks. The Procion inks used in this book are transparent and can be used to ink over dry varnish, dry acrylic or a medium such as a Paintstik. Dye powder may also be added directly to acrylic varnish or acrylic wax to create coloured media. The addition of water will dilute these mixtures, reducing their strength and changing their nature.
- **Brusho inks** These are powdered inks that can safely be used by children. The powders can be mixed with water to create rich intense colours. They can also be sprinkled directly on wet paper to create mottled effects. Brusho inks can be applied as inks or mixed with acrylics, and are used in just the same ways as Procion dyes.
- **Bronze and lustre powders** All bronze and lustre powders give metallic and iridescent finishes. Bronze powders are metal-based powders, while lustre powders are made of mica flakes; both should be treated with respect. All bronze and lustre powders must be mixed with a binder that will support the powder. Suitable binders include acrylic varnishes, and wax or texture gels, as well as various metallic binders. For further details see pages 70 and 78.

▲ Selection of powdered dyes.

◄ Acrylic jar colour with man-made and shaper brushes.

(Overleaf) Jars of bronze powders: bright silver (burnish) and light gold.

- **Acrylic paints** These are marketed in a wide range of products. Both tube and jar acrylic is used in this book. The jar colour tends to be thinner than tube colour and can easily be applied from a glass plate, roller or brush on any type of paper. Tube colour tends to be slightly heavier and stiffer, creating a medium that is thicker and stickier to apply and produces a slightly denser finish. There is a vast range of different acrylic media, including gels and pastes. They are made by a number of companies, such as Golden, Liquitex, Daler Rowney and Winsor and Newton. All companies offer excellent technical information, available from the addresses at the end of the book. Acrylic gels, pastes, varnishes and other media are all extensively used later in this book to create a variety of effects.

- **Markal Paintstiks (Shiva Paintstiks)** These are available in both iridescent and pure professional artist's colours, as well as a small fluorescent range. The pigment colour is mixed with either a mixture of pure oil-and-wax binder or with a pearlescent oil-and-wax binder and produced as a chunky crayon. This is wrapped in a card sleeve that protects the medium and makes it easy to handle. Paintstiks have a thick skin, which will need to be broken before use and will reseal, protecting the medium, after use. The range of 50 professional Paintstiks extends from dark rich colours, such as dioxazine purple, teal and ultramarine, to bright colours, such as azo yellow, yellow citron and cadmium orange. Colours such as mudstone, slate blue, and pewter grey include white, which makes them opaque and therefore useful for applying to dark backgrounds. Use the professional blender to extend colours, making them more transparent, or mix the iridescent blender with professional colours to create subtle pearl mixtures. Both blenders extend the colour, making it softer and easier to work. All Paintstiks, when applied in reasonable quantity, form excellent resists for water-based inks.

▶▶ (Above) Tubes of Pearlescent and Interference acrylic mediums. (Below) Professional Markal Paintstiks drawn onto Indian cotton rag paper.

▶ Selection of acrylic texture gels and pastes.

HEALTH AND SAFETY ADVICE

Care must be taken when mixing dye powders and bronze powders.

Powders should always be used with a binder or metallic medium.

When using the powders for preparation of inks, varnishes, or bronze or lustre finishes, always wear a mask and protective clothing, such as an apron and rubber gloves.

The necessary equipment should be kept especially for these media, and areas of preparation adequately covered with polythene or newspaper. Any mixture should be labelled and carefully stored.

Artist's materials, and their safe usage, are extensively documented in a variety of product literature published by the individual companies and some suppliers.

▶▶ Bronze powders: bright silver (burnish) and silver.

▼ Blocks of Formafoam and Speedy stamp, sheets of Foamtastic, craft knives and print rollers.

EQUIPMENT

The following equipment is very useful when creating glorious papers. It is not essential to have everything listed here, and in many cases substitutions can be made, but it will help you to achieve pleasing results with ease if you invest in some basic equipment. In addition to the equipment listed below, you will need a good craft knife or scalpel, a cutting board or mat, and a metal ruler.

- **Brushes** It pays to have a small range of different brushes: synthetic bristles are excellent with acrylics, but household paint brushes can be used as well. Sponge brushes are excellent for applying flat areas of thin, water-based colour. They come in four widths, and usually have black, blade-shaped sponge tips and wooden handles. It is useful to have six or seven of these brushes, one for each ink colour. It is also a good idea to have a shaper brush, which is a rubber-tipped brush that is ideal for drawing into wet surfaces.

- **A good palette** A radial one is a good choice, as is one with deep wells to contain inks.

- **A pair of toughened glass plates** These are used for printing; two sheets of laminated plastic are a good alternative.

- **A print roller** The type used for lino printing is a very useful tool, as it is excellent for applying colour rapidly to the glass plates and printing blocks.

- **Grouting tools** Combs of the type made for combing tile adhesive are used to make multiple lines.

- **Pump spray** This is a simple spray to be used with inks.

- **Foam core board** A lightweight board with a foam core, this is strong and durable, and is excellent as a base for blocks.

- **Foamtastic** This is a very thin, dense, brightly coloured foam that is easily cut with scissors or knife. It makes a good surface for patterns to be used for blocks.

  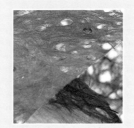 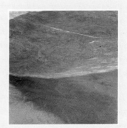

two
Colour and
Colour Mixing

Throughout this book, the illustrations are full of vivid colours that give a strength and richness to the surfaces and patterns. Being addicted to the use of colour is not harmful to your health, in fact the very opposite. You use colours to make you feel cheerful and excited, and even to stimulate your gastric juices!

Illustration: Fine lokta tissue painted with Procion dyes.

SUCCESSFUL COLOUR MIXING

The inks and dyes that have been used are taken from a very limited palette – lemon yellow, golden yellow, scarlet, magenta, ultramarine, turquoise and black. From these, a clean bright range of colours can be created. Care has to be taken not to drown the lighter colours – the yellows – with the heavier and more dominant colours, such as ultramarine and magenta. Sometimes it is necessary to dilute these heavier colours, as they can appear too dark, thus making it difficult to distinguish the different pinks, mauves, purples and violets.

▶ Colour spectrum painted with Procion dyes – lemon yellow, golden yellow, scarlet, magenta, ultramarine and turquoise.

▶▶ Lace papers painted with Procion dyes applied with a sponge brush.

▼ Kozo bamboo plait paper painted with Procion dyes.

When mixing colours, it is best to add dark to light colours. For example, start with yellow and add turquoise to create a range of citron, lime, emerald green and aquamarine. Remember that colours will always be darker when wet, so do not panic if a colour looks too dark initially!

Keep your brushes and any rinsing water clean; it is very easy for colours to become contaminated.

Finally, be aware that while your colours may appear to be red, yellow or blue, they will not be pure, and each will have a tendency towards another colour. Lemon yellow is a greenish yellow; golden yellow has a reddish tendency; scarlet has an orange tendency, while magenta leans

towards the purple or mauve colours. If you mix magenta and ultramarine you will create purple, but if you mix ultramarine, which is a violet blue, with scarlet, you will be more likely to get a deep brown than a strong purple. There is an element of yellow in the scarlet, and in mixing this with ultramarine it is easy to lean towards a tertiary colour, in this case brown.

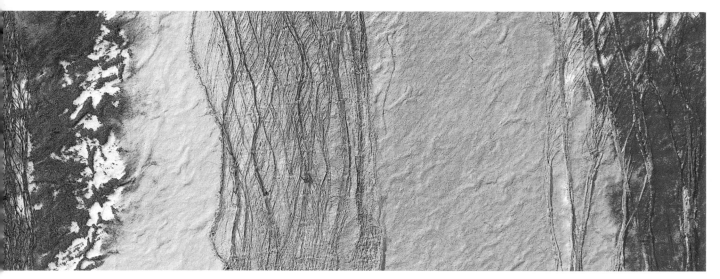

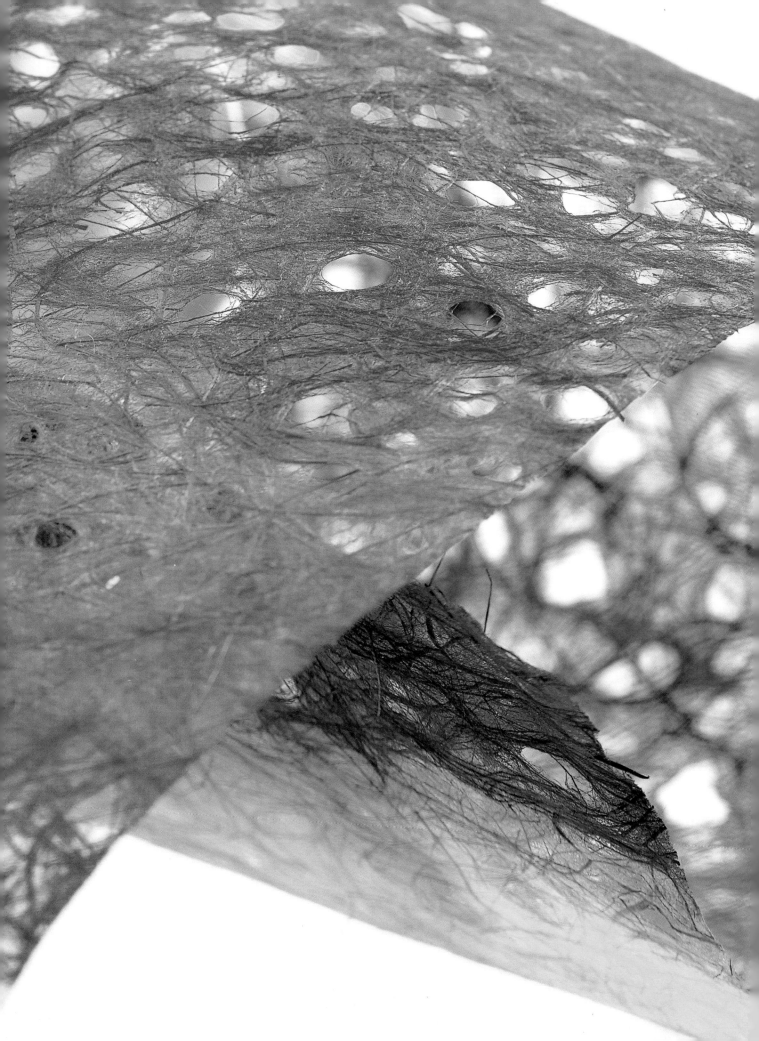

three
Painting Papers

Painting papers can be a wonderfully absorbing and relaxing occupation. For the papers featured here, diluted powdered dyes or Brusho ink are used, as these give brilliant transparent colours that can be applied with a paint brush, sponge or sponge brush.

Select a range of different types of papers. These might include commercially produced cartridge, watercolour and printer paper, a selection of handmade Asian papers, such as lokta tissue, Japanese lace and kozo papers, and even light card. When selecting your papers, spend time feeling the weight, softness, absorbency and the surface finish of the paper, as these factors will affect the painted result.

Illustration: Cotton rag paper with tea, painted with Procion dye applied with a fine brush.

PAINTING STRIPES

Try out the following experiments on a range of different papers, such as watercolour, Indian rag, photocopy and fine lokta, evaluating and analysing the results. When you have finished, leave the papers to dry and then review them later, adding more dye if you wish.

▼ Conqueror paper painted with Procion dye in stripes.

▶▼ Conqueror paper as a contact print from left.

MATERIALS

- selection of different papers, cut to a manageable size, such as A4, for experimentation
- palette of dyes or Brusho inks — select a balanced range of six or seven colours as outlined in the previous chapter
- newspaper to cover your work surface
- rubber gloves (as dye can stain your hands) and an apron
- brushes, such as synthetic sable, sponges cut into 2.5 cm (1 in) pieces and sponge brushes, which will absorb liquid colour. (It is useful to have one brush for each colour; continually washing the brushes is laborious and wet brushes tend to dilute the colours.)

METHOD

1 Take a medium-weight piece of cartridge paper; dip your brush into the lightest colour, and apply it gently and evenly across the paper.

2 Watch how the dye absorbs into the paper. Some papers will drink up the dye, leaving a matt surface on which brush marks can be seen. On finer finished papers the dye may lie on the surface for longer, sometimes creating a puddle.

3 Be aware of what is happening on your paper and use that to your advantage. If the colour is not absorbing into the paper quickly, use less dye or even blot the colour with another piece of paper.

4 Wet colour can be used to great effect if you lay one line of wet colour carefully alongside another, allowing them to bleed gently into each other.

5 Sometimes a colour will run across a number of other colours, creating a very dramatic effect.

6 Continue laying rows of colour adjacent to each other, until you have a beautiful rainbow paper.

7 If the surface of the paper is very damp, but not awash with dye, carefully place a clean sheet of paper over it. Gently press the two together and immediately peel them apart. The result is often a beautiful paper, which has taken up the excess dye, giving it a delicate dotted surface, sometimes representing clouds or skies.

CRUMPLED PAPERS

Using the same materials as for painting stripes, select a range of fine absorbent papers: for example, cartridge, brown and commercial printer paper, such as Conqueror. Choose a paper that will crease when you screw it up in your hand; some thicker papers almost crack, giving them a leather-like surface.

◀ Conqueror paper, crumpled, repeatedly inked with red, yellow and turquoise dyes.

METHOD

1 Moisten your brush with the chosen dye colour. Make sure that the brush is not saturated, as it only needs to be damp.

2 Lightly move the brush across the crumpled surface of the paper, leaving some areas undyed.

3 Allow the paper to dry before applying another colour.

4 Repeat the applications of dye, maybe screwing the paper again so that other areas are coloured.

5 If the paper starts to tear, allow the dye to dry thoroughly before further applications of colour.

6 On some papers, the dye will penetrate through the paper, creating attractive effects on the reverse side.

7 By placing a clean sheet of paper on the wet surface of the crumpled paper, a contact print of the ridge patterns can be obtained.

Try the above on a number of different papers and compare the results. If the entire surface of a paper is coloured, you are either applying the colour too heavily or the brush is too wet with dye.

▼ The reverse side of inked and crumpled paper after repeated applications of dye.

SPRAYED PAPERS

(Preceding page)
Lightweight card
sprayed with a range
of Procion dyes.

Either a pump spray or diffuser may be used to spray the dye on paper. By using a fine spray, you can gradually build up the colour to create very subtle and blended changes. It saves time to have a spray bottle or diffuser for each colour and enables you to mix colours quickly and create the effect you want.

MATERIALS

- palette of dyes or Brusho inks – select a balanced range of six or seven colours as outlined in the previous chapter
- newspaper to cover your work surface
- rubber gloves
- selection of thick or absorbent papers
- pump sprays or diffusers

METHOD

1 The chosen paper should be thick or absorbent, as it will become very damp during spraying.

2 Care needs to be taken not to get the surface too saturated as this results in pools of colour, which can be unattractive.

3 It is possible to spray on a horizontal surface, but take care to cover the surrounding area with newspaper.

4 Spray the surface of the paper with a selection of colours, taking care not to saturate any particular area.

5 To retain the definition of the colours and to prevent them becoming muddy, allow the paper to dry between different applications.

6 It is possible to place a temporary mask, such as torn paper, on the surface of the paper during spraying. In this way, the colours can be layered up, creating lines of colour.

▶ Cotton rag paper with straw, painted with Procion dye, the side tip of a sponge brush being used to create triangular shapes.

▶▶ Lokta wood dust paper painted with various Procion dye colours.

f o u r
Resists and Inks

The term resist refers to a medium that is applied to a surface to protect it

from further additions of wet colour. Batik, for example, is a resist method in

which a fabric is painted with a design in hot wax to prevent the absorption

of dye into the fibres at the waxed areas. Similar effects can be created on

paper, where inks and resists can be combined to add an extra dimension to

your creations, producing some unexpected and dramatic results.

Illustration: Watercolour paper painted with Procion dyes and worked with professional Paintstiks.

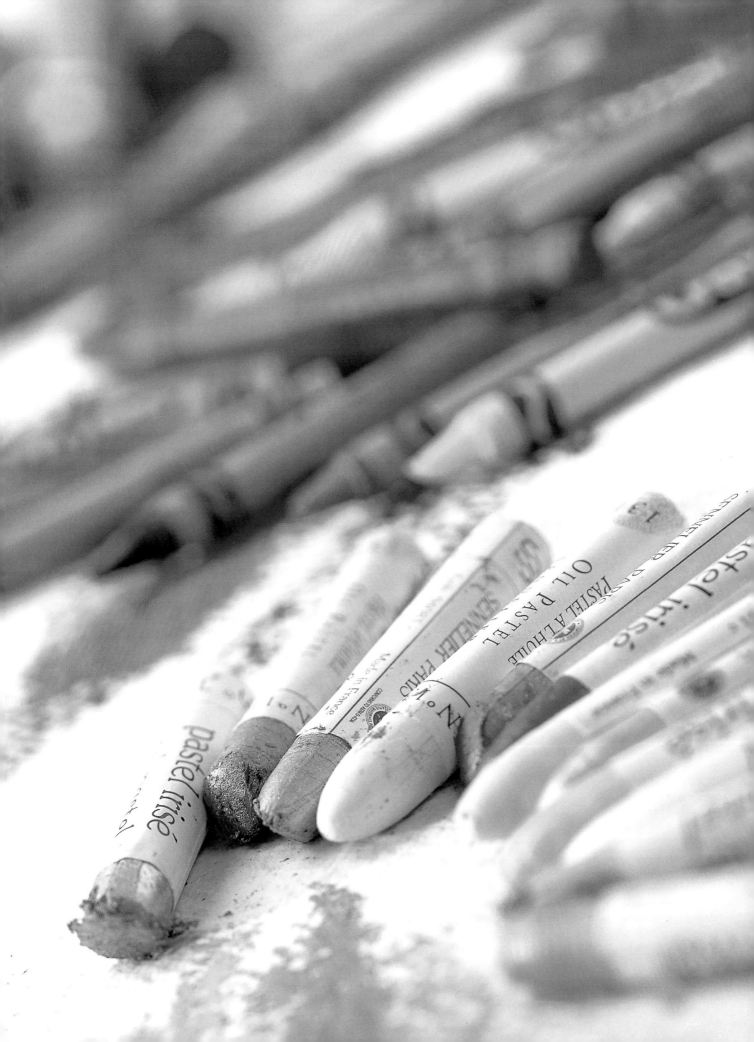

RESISTS

The following materials can be used as a resist on paper – oil pastels, wax crayons, wax candles and Paintstiks. All these media come in stick form, with varying amounts of colour or pigment, and even – in some cases – the option of an iridescent binder.

Each make and type will vary in nature from the rest: oil pastels are rich with colour and have a slightly sticky quality, whereas Paintstiks are soft smooth oil-and-wax crayon that are rich in pigment. Other wax crayons, and also candles, will be hard, thus giving the opportunity to create much harder lines with less intensity of colour. The softer oilier media will pick up all the textures in the paper surface or can easily be spread in a smooth coating, especially on a fine finished surface.

Sennelier iridescent oil pastels and the iridescent Paintstiks can be applied to darker papers to create beautiful shimmering pearl effects.

All the above will work with any water-based ink, such as Brusho or Procion dye, as well as some commercial inks. Certain commercial inks, however, contain shellac or acrylic, which may adhere to the resist and spoil the finished effect.

OIL AND WAX RESISTS

The following effects can be produced with a variety of oil and wax resists, ranging from Paintstiks, Sennelier oil pastels, wax crayons and oil pastels to wax candles.

MATERIALS
- papers – both smooth types, such as cartridge or commercial printer paper, and rough, textured papers, such as Indian cotton rag with tea or Himalayan rough lokta
- oil pastels, such as Sennelier iridescent pastels, wax crayons, candles, and Paintstiks, especially the blenders (professional or iridescent)
- prepared inks, either Procion dyes or Brusho inks
- paint brushes and/or sponge brushes

METHOD
1 Take any of the oil or wax crayons and draw simple lines on your paper. You will find that it is easy to draw on a smooth paper, whereas you will require a softer crayon, such as a Paintstik, for the roughly textured papers.

▲ Procion dyes were painted on different types of cotton rag paper (banana and tea) and lokta huck. Professional and iridescent Paintstiks were then worked into the dry surfaces.

◀◀ Selection of wax crayons and Sennelier oil pastels.

41

2　Try using the side of a candle to make wide lines and broad sweeps, or use a series of wax crayons to build up layers of colour. Ink over these wax media to create a broken inked surface.

3　If you draw on coloured cotton rag paper with the creamy Sennelier iridescent oil pastels, you will produce a textured effect that is almost spotty in appearance.

4　Paint over the oil or wax crayons with the inks or dyes and watch the former resist the colour.

5　Once the ink is dry, further layers of oil or wax can be added to build up the colours.

▼ Iridescent Sennelier oil pastels on cotton rag paper.

◄ Conqueror paper was painted with stripes of Procion dyes and left to dry; Paintstik professional blender was then used to draw on the paper, after which it was further painted with dyes.

(Overleaf) Professional Paintstik colours were mixed on paper with a blending stick and the paper was then inked with Procion dyes.

▶ This painting of a
barn wall was made
with Procion dyes and
a blending stick on
watercolour paper.

FURTHER EFFECTS

Markal (Shiva) blending sticks can be used with precision. Working on watercolour paper with Procion dyes, first paint with dye. Next, mask areas with the blender, and then paint the paper with further dye. The blender will remain transparent but will protect the initial layers of colour from the second application.

Using a craft knife, try scratching back into the resists, especially when these have been applied to a heavyweight paper; the etching will give depth and texture to the surface.

Another option is to place a paper – for example, fine lokta tissue, printer paper, or Japanese Gampi – on a textured surface or printing block, and then make a rubbing of the pattern or texture. Paintstiks give excellent rubbings, especially when the colour is gently stroked across the surface of the paper. The rubbing can be done repeatedly and then inked over.

▼ Professional Paintstik colour was rubbed over a block covered with lokta fine tissue paper, which had previously been painted with Procion dyes.

RESISTS WITH ACRYLIC VARNISH OR WAX

Acrylic varnish and acrylic wax create a totally different resist as they are liquids and only act as a resist once they are dry. When these products are wet, they appear opaque and milky. Once dry, they become clear, transparent or translucent, with either matt or shiny finishes.

Acrylic wax and acrylic varnish are both used in the same way, but the wax gives a more subtle finish, with a slightly waxy surface. If the wax is used, the colours will be less intense because the wax stays slightly cloudy. Acrylic varnish is completely transparent when dry, and can give a gloss or matt finish.

Both the acrylic wax and the varnish can be used on many porous surfaces, including plaster, untreated wood and unglazed terracotta, as well as fabric and paper.

MATERIALS
- lightweight papers, such as greaseproof, tissue, fine lokta, Japanese Gampi and mulberry tissue
- medium and heavier papers, such as cartridge, Indian cotton rag papers and rough lokta
- gloss acrylic varnish and/or acrylic wax
- powdered dyes or Brusho
- sponge brushes and paint brushes
- protective mask
- small plastic dishes

METHOD
1 Remember to wear a mask if you are mixing dye powders, and use small plastic dishes to mix as many colours as you require. Mix a small amount (as little as quarter of a teaspoon) of dye powder or Brusho into acrylic varnish or wax. Make sure the dye powder is well mixed into the varnish, and that all the grains are dissolved.

2 Always check the strength of your colour before beginning a piece of work. Take care not to add too much water or the varnish may be too runny. Experiment with different ways of applying the varnish, using the methods described below.

◀ Sponge brushes were used to apply successive layers of gloss varnish and Procion dye to cartridge paper.

▼ Acrylic varnish mixed with Brusho powdered inks and printed on cartridge paper with rectangles of sponge. Once dry, the paper was coloured with turquoise Brusho ink.

49

▲◀ Procion dye powder was mixed with gloss acrylic varnish, painted in layers, and drawn into with a grouting tool; a further layer was then added.

▲▶ In a sketch book, acrylic varnish and Procion dyes were used to document different bead arrangements found in African necklaces.

▼◀ Matt and gloss acrylic varnishes were mixed with dye powder and painted on Kozo bamboo stripe paper.

▼▶ Gloss varnish was mixed with Procion dye powder and layered with a brush on fine lokta tissue paper.

3　Small pieces of sponge may be dipped into the different colours of varnish and printed on the paper.

4　Paint the coloured varnish across the paper, and then, while it is still wet, draw into the surface with grouting tools, palette knives, or combs. The marks will create a slight surface pattern. Allow the varnish to dry, and then repeat the process with a second colour.

5　Using a separate brush for each colour of varnish, apply the colours in any order, painting one on top of another. The transparent colours will combine to create a wonderful depth, especially if each colour is allowed to dry before the next is applied.

6　Use a colourless varnish to coat specific areas of a previously dyed paper in order to seal them, then ink over the entire surface of the paper to change the colour of the unvarnished areas.

USEFUL TIPS

The following points are always worth remembering when using acrylic varnish or wax.

- Acrylic wax or varnish can be coloured before use with a water-based colour, such as ink, dye, or Brusho.
- Dye or Brusho can also be added in powder form to create excellent coloured varnishes and waxes.
- Once dry, an acrylic will resist other water-based liquids, such as inks.
- Acrylic varnish will dry to a transparent finish and can thus be used to 'seal' an area before you add more ink.
- Both acrylic wax and acrylic varnish can be used as transparent or translucent binders for bronze and lustre powders (see page 80).

▲ Mulberry tissue and silk paper were painted with Procion dyes. Gloss acrylic varnish was then used to laminate the silk paper to the mulberry tissue.

FURTHER EFFECTS

Each type of paper will react in a different way to acrylic varnish: greaseproof will cockle slightly, handmade papers will reveal all their unusual fibres, fine lokta tissue will become like a transparent fabric. Contrasting surfaces can be created: for example, shiny paper with matt inked areas, cockled areas with flat satin acrylic wax, and richly grooved surfaces with contrasting layers of patterned coloured varnishes. Each paper will be different, and every application will produce a specific response; some you will like, and others will need to be set aside for further work!

LAYERING WITH VARNISH

Once you have created some papers, you may wish to begin to layer them together. Layering techniques are very effective when used with the finer papers, such as commercial tissue, fine lokta tissue, silk papers, mulberry tissue or handmade Japanese papers.

Every addition of acrylic wax or varnish strengthens the surface, giving the opportunity to make papers that are delicate yet strong. As you apply your chosen acrylic coating, you will find that this does not make the paper stiffer; instead, it remains flexible and can easily be manipulated and even stitched. Very attractive and colourful results can be produced with the methods described below.

▸▸ Laid lokta, Japanese Gampi and lace paper were all painted with acrylic varnishes, both matt and gloss. They were glued together with uncoloured varnish, after which it remained possible to manipulate the papers, creating additional surface interest.

- Papers can be cut or torn, placed on a plain or decorated paper, and then varnished into position.
- Some papers become more transparent when varnished on both sides, and will bond extremely well with the background paper.
- Papers can either be applied flat, or ruched or gathered into position for added surface interest.
- Further layers of paper or additional coats of varnish or wax can be added to build up the surface.

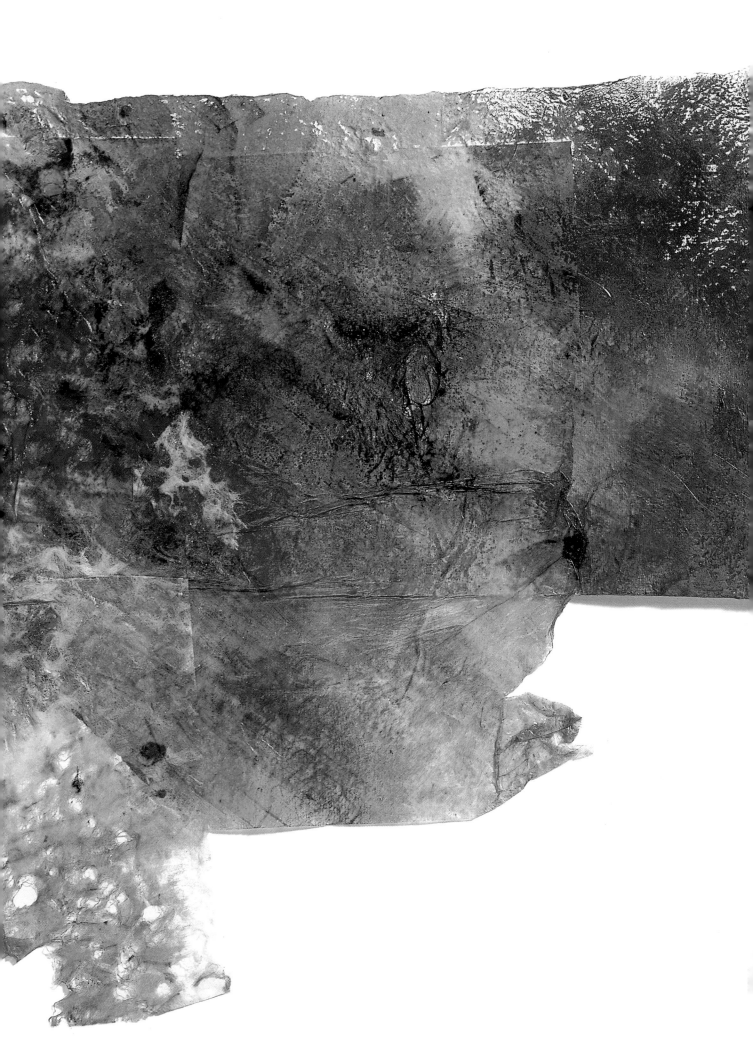

five
Printing Papers

Acrylic paint is an ideal medium for all types of printing. In the form of a jar colour, it will spread easily and yet, when drawn into, will remain static. The tube colour is slightly firmer, producing a thicker, more raised effect. When choosing which type of acrylic to use, the weight and density of your paper is an important consideration.

Acrylic colours vary in their quality; some products are very rich in pigment colour, whereas others lack vibrancy and depth. When using acrylic paints, remember the advice given earlier about mixing colours, and select a limited palette. Mix colours carefully, as it is very easy to create heavy muddy colours; these can be depressing and are very wasteful.

Illustration: Light violet, light purple and cadmium yellow acrylic jar colour block-and-roller printed from a hand-cut lino block. Once dry, the prints were painted with magenta dye.

GLASS-PLATE PRINTING

▶▶ Acrylic colour and white were applied to a glass plate with a roller. The surface was drawn into with circular movements by a shaper brush and the plate was printed on medium lokta paper. This technique was then repeated and, when dry, the print was inked with lemon yellow and magenta dye.

Toughened glass or firm plastic sheets provide a very quick and accessible surface on which to draw and design patterns, and can result in highly successful prints. Keep designs simple at the beginning; they will soon become complex with the addition of more printing and colours!

If early attempts result in rather heavy prints and the colour has spread, this simply means that you have applied either too much paint or too much pressure. Do not be downhearted if initial prints are not as you want: make some more, exploring different methods, colours and papers. Try not to be too critical at this stage. Initial disasters can often be transformed with more printing and inking into much-loved pieces!

MATERIALS
* acrylic colour – tube or jar
* toughened glass or stiff laminated plastic sheet
* print roller or broad paint brush
* grouting tools, shaper brushes, combs or similar items for drawing (etching)
* smooth papers that will give quality prints – commercial machine-made papers, smooth cotton rag, fine smooth lokta and Thai papers

METHOD
1. Coat the surface evenly with acrylic colour, spreading it with either a wide brush or a rubber roller.
2. Draw into the surface with any simple item, such as a stick, a piece of dowel, an old cork, a shaper brush or a piece of plastic.
3. Draw simple patterns – lines, circles, wavy lines or zigzags – across the painted surface.
4. Select a sheet of paper to fit your painted area; place the paper face down on the painted surface, and gently press to obtain a print.

▶ Yellow acrylic jar colour was printed on cartridge paper with a glass plate. Once dry, the print was painted with mixtures of magenta, turquoise, ultramarine and lemon yellow dyes. It was finally coated with gloss varnish.

5   Carefully peel off your paper and lay it out to dry. (Alternatively, a print can be obtained by placing the glass plate on the paper.)

6   Once the first print is dry, you can either leave it as it is, perhaps adding ink at a later stage, or print over it again, using other colours to build up more complex patterns and surfaces.

FURTHER EFFECTS

When creating a more complex printed paper, it is a good idea to use the same type of shapes repeatedly. If you have already printed circles, for example, add more circles rather than moving to a different pattern, such as one formed from straight lines.

You may be able to avoid washing the plate between prints if you plan the sequence of colour changes. Start with a mixture of turquoise and white, for example; print; add some magenta to change the colour to a light blue/violet; print again; add further magenta to make the colour more violet; print again; add more magenta to produce a purple colour, and so on. Unusual and original colour combinations can be made by mixing colours in this way. Sometimes the colours will become layered on the plate, resulting in a print of layered colours.

Use a range of implements to make multiple lines and create patterns quickly. Old combs, forks and grouting tools (spreaders for tile adhesive) can all be used to produce parallel lines on your glass plate, or you can make your own tool by cutting notches into stiff plastic or acetate.

▶▶ Acrylic colour was lightly applied across the surface of Indian coloured ruched paper.

▼ Light lokta paper was sprayed with turquoise and ultramarine dye. Once dry, the paper was printed with a glass plate covered with scarlet and yellow acrylic colour that had been drawn into.

ROLLER PRINTING

A hard rubber print roller is a useful tool, as it will help you to spread the acrylic quickly and evenly on the glass plate. When you apply the acrylic to the plate, the roller will sometimes create little ripples of colour, especially if the thicker acrylic is being used, and with care these ripples can be printed from roller to paper.

PRINTING TIPS

- Ensure that there is sufficient acrylic on the glass plate – too little and the roller will not turn, too much and the roller will slip and become ineffective.
- Do not press too hard or the roller will not rotate.
- If you gently guide the roller backwards and forwards, supporting the handle in the palm of your hand, you will find that it will move easily.
- Gently roll the colour onto your paper – the pressure required will depend on the weight of the paper and the amount of colour on your roller.
- Watch how the colour is transferring to the paper and adjust the pressure accordingly.

PRINTING BLOCKS

Blocks offer another quick way to create multiple images, enabling you to develop design ideas in a variety of different styles, colours and arrangements. To create a very simple block, take a piece of thick card or core board

and use good quality double-sided tape to attach an assortment of different items to the surface. Blocks of this type are very durable, and an application of acrylic will help to seal the surface.

Any of the following materials or objects will make excellent surfaces for blocks: old mouse mats, thick polystyrene packing (used to pack fruit), Foamtastic (a very thin foam sheet) or Neoprene (wet-suit fabric). All of these can be cut into shape and adhered to core board with double-sided tape. Various cheap plastic household items – tile spacers, plant ties and plastic washers, for example – create interesting patterns when placed repeatedly across a square block.

Firm string or lightweight cord may be formed into linear patterns, but ensure that the surface is as level as possible and that the string is sufficiently strong to resist being flattened during printing.

After you have tried out some prints with the basic method, you might like to experiment with less usual glass-plate and roller printing methods, both of which will dramatically alter the printed appearance of the block on paper.

MATERIALS

- acrylic colours
- card or core board
- double-sided tape
- cut shapes, small plastic items, and/or string or cord

SIMPLE METHOD

1 Having made the block, apply plenty of acrylic colour to the surface. This helps the surface items to adhere more strongly and improves the print quality.
2 Try the block in a variety of different arrangements: formal lines, offset slightly to one side, rotated to create different directional movements, over-printed with different colours.
3 When printing is completed, wipe the block to remove the excess colour, but avoid soaking the block in water, as this will weaken the adhesion.

glorious papers

(Preceding page, clockwise from top left) Roller print from a block made of tile spacers, printed on coloured lokta paper with Interference acrylic tube colour; String block print using acrylic colour with additions of yellow and black ink; Block print made from plant ties, using white and lilac acrylic on laid lokta paper, inked with yellow and scarlet ink; Block with spirals of Foamtastic, impressed into the glass plate, then printed and inked on light lokta.

▶ A spiral block print from a glass-plate impression on light lokta paper; the second print has been painted with orange dye.

GLASS-PLATE METHOD

1   Apply acrylic colour evenly to a glass plate.
2   Impress the block repeatedly across the surface. This will leave an image of the pattern, plus other surface patterning, depending on the design of the block.
3   Place the paper on the plate, taking care not to press too hard and lose the more subtle effects of the acrylic.

ROLLER PRINTING METHOD

1   Cover the roller with acrylic by rolling it on a glass plate, making sure the colour is evenly distributed.
2   Roll across the surface of the block, observing the patterns appearing on the surface of the roller. Each time the roller is moved across the block, the pattern will become more complex.
3   Gently roll this more complex pattern onto the paper – the first revolution of the roller will give a clear print, while the second will be lighter as there will be less acrylic on the roller.
4   By taking the roller across the block at an angle, a different arrangement is obtained. A block with tile spacers has a square mesh; roll this type of block diagonally to create a diamond grid that may look like fish scales or a snakeskin pattern.
5   If it is first heavily covered with acrylic colour, it is possible to make a roller skid across the paper, producing a distorted version of the block design.

ADDING INKS TO PRINTS

Once the paper prints are dry, they can be painted with inks or dyes. Apply the ink or dye with either a paint brush or a sponge brush, enhancing areas that either lack colour or need an element of contrast.

The ink may stain the acrylic colour; if you wish to maintain the original effect in some parts, blot these areas immediately with kitchen towel.

Acrylic prints can be transformed with a wash of ink. The inks are most effective when used on paper that is white or light, although more muted effects can be obtained when ink is painted over lightly coloured papers, such as greys, light blues and greens.

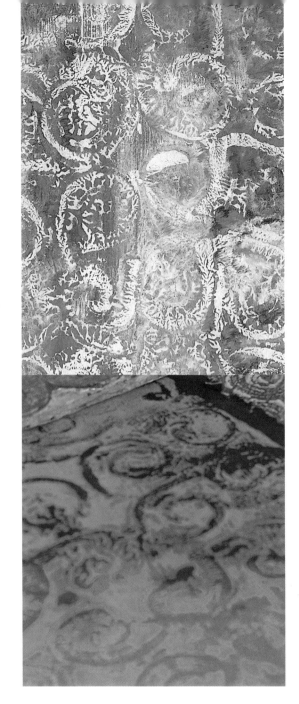

FURTHER EFFECTS

•   On dark papers, mix the acrylic colours with iridescent tinting medium or pearlescent colours, which will be visible on dark grounds.
•   On coloured papers, the addition of white acrylic will often make the colours glow, and will give extra vibrancy to the colours when they are inked over.
•   Prints on coloured paper are useful for torn-paper designs, as the papers will reveal coloured edges.

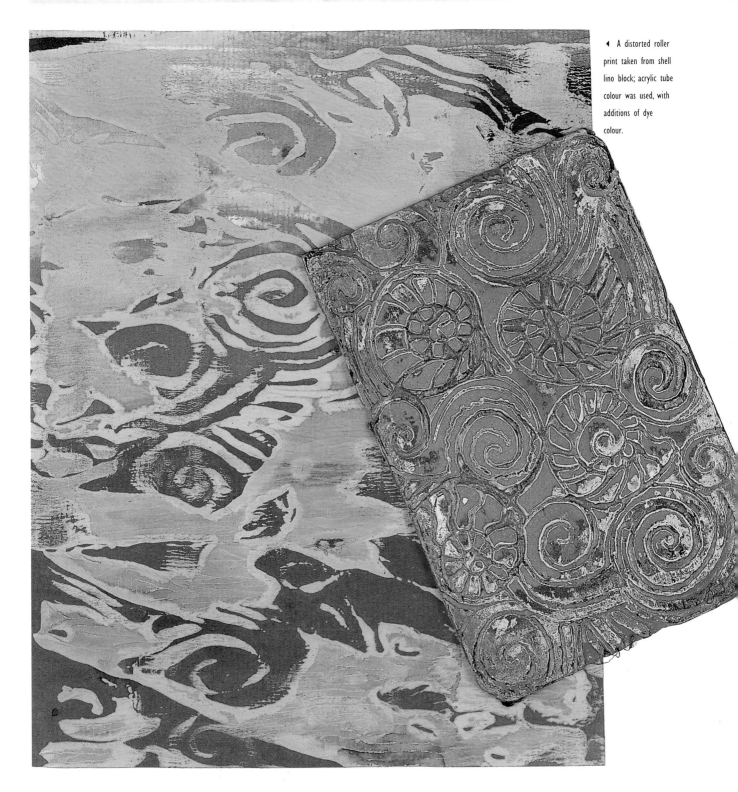

◀ A distorted roller print taken from shell lino block; acrylic tube colour was used, with additions of dye colour.

  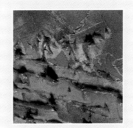 

six

Texture Gels

Texture gels are acrylic media into which you can mix any water-based colours, such as acrylics, inks, and dyes, as well as metallic powders. Available in a range of different surface finishes – rough, smooth, opaque or transparent – they offer a wonderful selection of surface finishes.

These gels can prove a very useful aid to the realization of design ideas; they add dimension to a design, producing some amazing effects in themselves.

When the gels are mixed with colour, inked and rubbed with Paintstiks, the results can be very dramatic.

Illustration: Extra heavy gel medium was mixed with magenta dye and with iridescent gold acrylic colour. The resulting gels were applied with a palette knife; once the gels were fully dry, further additions of Procion dye colour were made.

GEL TYPES

Acrylic texture gels are usually sold in small dumpy jars. Initially, they appear white and opaque, but once applied to paper and left to dry (if the gel is thickly applied, this can take up to 12 hours), their appearance will alter. The acrylic binder is so thick that it is possible to use the gel to create coloured and raised surfaces. With textures that may include tiny glass beads, mica flakes or extra coarse granules, the gels offer the opportunity to devise exotic and rich crunchy surfaces.

Texture gels are available in both matt and shiny finishes, as well as opaque and transparent ones. It is important to read the label on the jar, as this will describe the texture and finish of the gel when dry. For instance, white opaque flakes, suspended in a transparent gel, will give a flecked effect, whereas other gels, such as heavy gel medium, will dry to a clear glossy finish.

The following finishes are available: heavy gel, extra heavy gel, extra coarse granular gel, clear tar gel, pumice gel, garnet gel, as well as gel with gold, pearl and mica flakes.

Further gels include natural sand, resin sand, ceramic stucco, glass beads, black lava, white opaque flakes, blended fibres, and black mica.

▶ A selection of texture gels appear opaque when taken from the pot; no colour has been added to these gels and some will become transparent as they dry.

▶▶ Glass bead texture gel was mixed with interference red, and applied to a watercolour paper with a bristle brush and a palette knife. Once dry, the paper and gel were inked with Procion dyes.

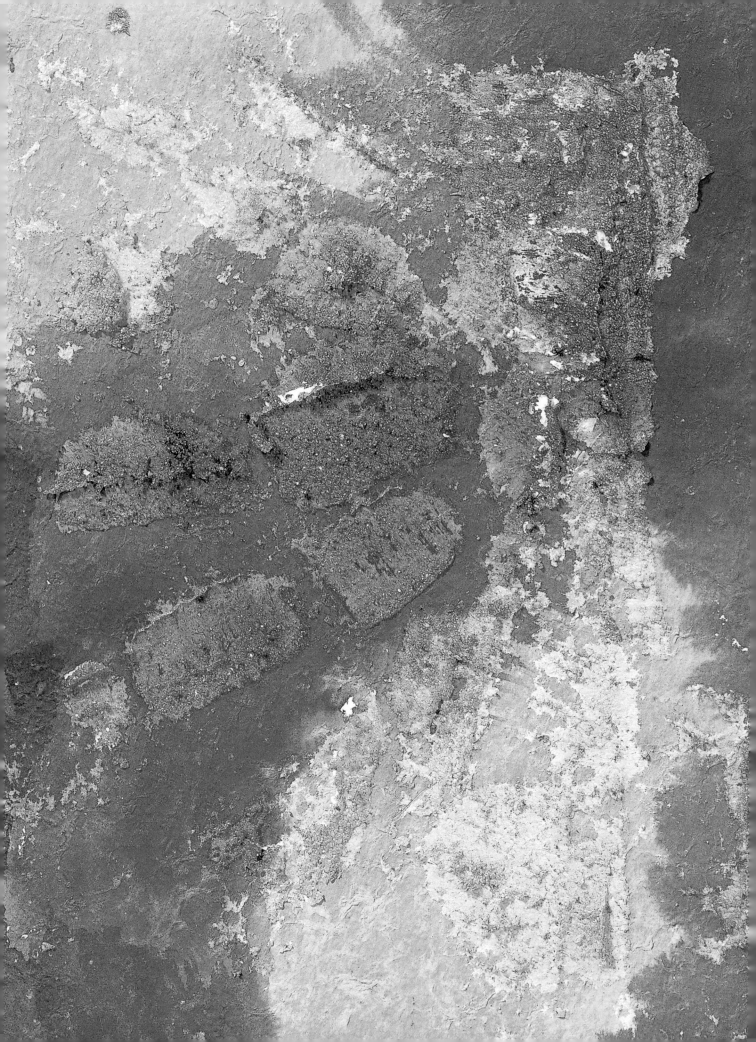

COLOURING TEXTURE GELS

When colouring gels, bear in mind that any added liquid will reduce the thickness of the gel and therefore its ability to produce raised surfaces. If you are adding inks, dyes or Brusho, try to use as little liquid as possible; an alternative is to mix in a small quantity of dye or Brusho powder. This will create a richly coloured gel, often transparent, which can then be applied to paper. The addition of acrylic colour to a gel will also give a rich colour, but will tend to make the gel slightly more opaque.

To add bronze and lustre powders (see also pages 19 and 78) to texture gels, carefully measure out a small amount – half a teaspoon – of the chosen powder and fold this into about 2 tbsp (just over 30 ml) of texture gel. Ensure that the powder is well mixed in and is totally absorbed into the gel. It may be necessary to add further quantities of powder, depending on the required strength of metallic or lustre sheen.

A mixture of gold bronze powder and heavy gel will look dull and matt when wet, but as it dries the mixture will become transparent, revealing the sheen and depth of the bronze powder.

▶▶ Heavy gel was mixed with a very small quantity of scarlet dye and glass-plate printed on light card. Once dry, the surface was painted first with golden yellow and with ultramarine dye, the dye being allowed to colour some of the gel surfaces as well as the paper.

▶ A texture gel – a mixture of opaque white flakes and interference green acrylic was applied with brush, stick and palette knife to a lightweight card. Once dry this was painted with Procion dyes, the colour being worked over both the gel and the paper surfaces.

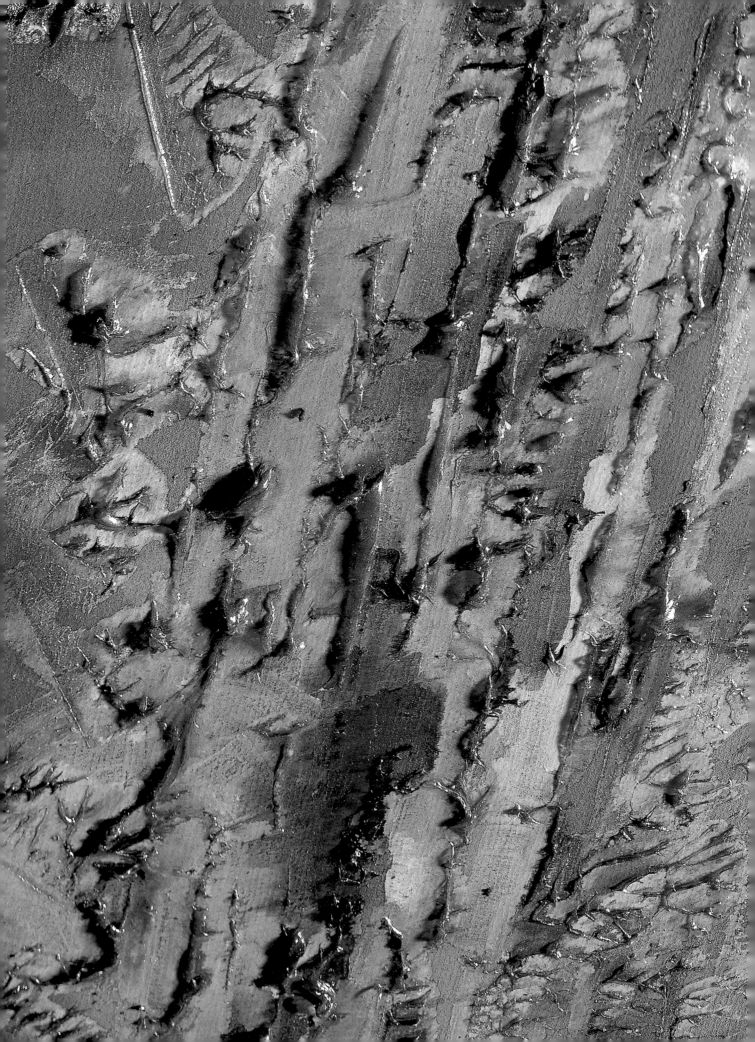

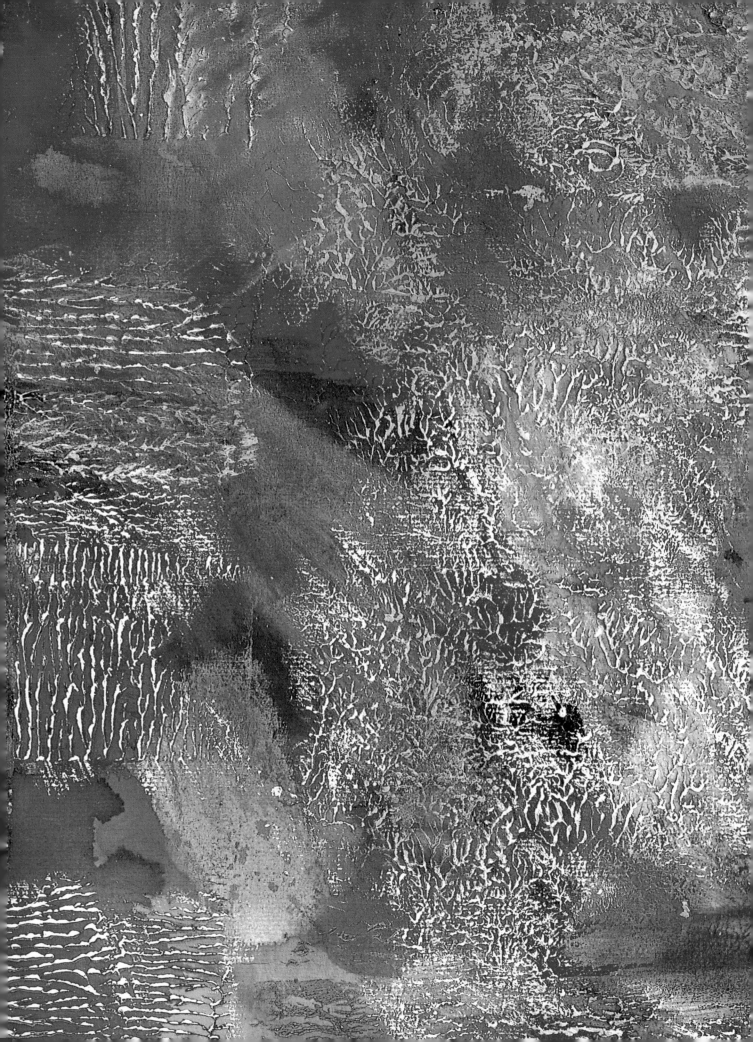

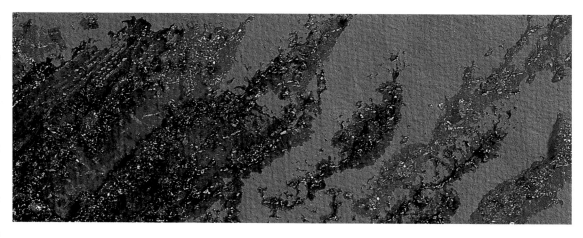

▶ Extra-coarse granular gel was mixed with small quantities of turquoise and lemon yellow dye powder, to create a lime green. This was applied to terracotta Indian rag paper with a knife. When wet, the gel was bright and opaque, but after 24 hours it had dried to a transparent gel, displaying the qualities of the coarse granular texture.

(Preceding page) Heavyweight cartridge paper was printed with iridescent copper acrylic mixed into a heavy gel medium. The colour was applied with roller, block and glass-plate printing. Once dry, the paper was painted with dyes; some areas were varnished, and these were then further inked. Finally, areas were rubbed lightly with a Paintstik to emphasize the textures and patterns created by printing with the heavy gel.

HEALTH AND SAFETY

When mixing any powdered dyes, bronze or lustre powders, it is important to wear a mask and rubber gloves and to use equipment kept for this purpose.

APPLYING TEXTURE GELS

These stiff, heavy gels require firm application. Select the paper carefully, choosing a slightly thicker type, such as a light card, heavy cartridge or stout Indian cotton rag paper.

To apply the gels, use a palette knife, spatula or roller, or apply them from a glass plate. Printing with the gels can be very rewarding, as the gels will mould, curl and model happily (see photograph on page 69).

Some of the rough gels, however – for example, the ceramic stucco, resin sand, glass beads and the coarse gritty types – are difficult to print from a glass plate, and the noise of the textures scratching on the glass can be unpleasant!

If you are using a brush to apply the gels, choose one that has stiff bristles, and work the gel into the paper, emphasizing the surface created with the brush.

Stencilling can be a very satisfactory technique to use with texture gel, as the stencil will give a distinct edge to the gel shape so that the texture of the gel can be fully appreciated.

ADDING INKS OR DYES

When dry, the coloured gels sometimes lack variety and depth. This can be remedied by applying areas of dye to both the texture gel and the background paper. The dye can adhere to the surface and transform it; dye may also seep under the edges of the gel, colouring the paper where the gel has been scraped thin. This adds a further dimension to the surface of the paper, creating a whole range of unusual and unexpected effects.

EFFECTS WITH PAINTSTIKS

Once dry, the surface of texture gels can be enhanced with Paintstiks. Their oily nature and the high quality of the pigment colour make the latter easy to apply. It is always surprising that an oil-and-wax medium such as this can be applied to a dry acrylic surface and yet be fully absorbed after about 48 hours.

When a Paintstik is rubbed lightly across the textured surface, the colour will adhere to the raised areas,

emphasizing the pattern. Certain texture gels – for example, ceramic stucco, black mica, resin sand, pumice and garnet gels – are particularly suited to this treatment (see photograph on pages 70-1).

With other gels, such as natural sand and heavy gel, attractive effects are obtained by carefully rubbing with a Paintstik. Work the colour into the surface so as to pick up all the little ripples and surface variations.

COMBINING COLOUR AND TEXTURE

Texture gels offer an ideal starting point for the creation of a multi-textured, coloured and lustrous paper.

MATERIALS

- heavyweight paper, such as a light card or a sheet of Indian cotton rag paper
- acrylic iridescent bronze
- heavy gel
- dye(s)
- acrylic gloss or matt varnish
- Paintstiks – professional and iridescent colour
- roller
- palette knife
- two glass plates

METHOD

1 Mix some acrylic iridescent bronze and heavy gel (gloss) on a glass plate with a palette knife.

2 Using a printing roller, roll the colour until it is evenly spread, coating the roller. Ripples of colour will form on the roller, and this effect can be transferred to the paper by gently rolling it across the surface of the paper.

3 Further patterns can be created by placing two glass plates together, squeezing the heavy gel. Prise the plates apart with a round-bladed knife and a fernlike pattern will appear. Gently print the pattern on the paper, watching through the glass to ensure that you do not flatten the raised surface.

4 Further additions of heavy gel and bronze iridescent acrylic may be necessary. In order to get the full benefit of the textures, it is important to be fairly generous with these gels.

5 The gel will take between one and 12 hours to dry, depending on the thickness of application.

6 Once a gel is fully dry, the paper and gel can be painted with dye mixed with gloss or matt varnish.

7 Allow the dyed areas to dry. These areas can then be further enhanced with blending sticks, iridescent Paintstiks, or even further applications of dye and acrylic varnish. These applications will all add depth and intrigue.

8 Finally, the raised surfaces of the ripples of gel can be highlighted with a rubbing of light-coloured Professional Paintstik, such as light green or ice blue.

▲ Iridescent gold acrylic was mixed with heavy gel and applied with a wooden kebab stick to a paper sprayed with dye. Further applications of middle gold bronze powder and green lustre powder, mixed with extra coarse pumice gel, were made using a palette knife and the kebab stick.

73

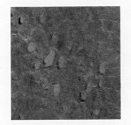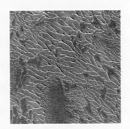

seven

Metallic Effects

Metallic effects on paper can create magical shimmering surfaces, ranging from glitters and sheen to the more subtle finishes of pearlescents and lustres. They are available as powders, to be mixed with a binder, or a jar or tube colour, or even a wax and oil stick. Worked into a dark and textured paper they become irresistible.

Illustration: Roller print using pearl lustre powders mixed with a gel medium and applied to Keaykolour paper, which has fine mica flakes embedded in the surface of the paper.

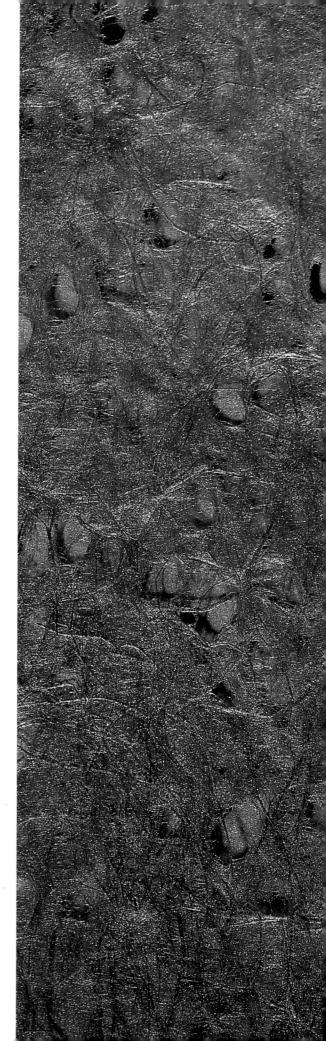

METALLIC BRONZE AND LUSTRE POWDERS

In recent years, there has been a huge increase in the variety of metallic and lustre powders available, and it is now possible to purchase silver, any number of golds, and coppers, as well as shimmering pearls, glitter reds and duo colours.

Bronze powders have a metal base and are available in a range of gold, coppers and silver, as well as some metallic colours, such as mauve, green and blue. When dry, they will give a rich and shiny metallic surface. Fire copper, for example, is a warm red copper colour, while middle gold is a greenish gold.

Lustre and pearl powders are not metal-based, but are made from mica flakes that have been treated to create all kinds of mysterious colourings. These range from pearl colours that resemble delicate flakes of shell in pinks, lilacs, greens and blues, to more robust iridescent effects, such as lustre copper, glitter red and shimmering gold. These lustre powders do not shine like the metal powders, but create rich reflective colours and luscious finishes.

There are also dual lustre colours, including Pearl Ex, that have two contrasting lustres mixed together, such as gold green, pink blue or blue green. For example, when a paper is moved one way, a patch of colour may appear green, while the same area will appear golden when the paper is turned the other way, in an effect similar to the plumage of an exotic bird.

▶ Japanese lace paper and brown wrapping paper were brushed with light gold bronze powder, lilac lustre powder and green/gold Pearl Ex lustre powder mixed with acrylic varnish. Although the same metallic and lustre powders were used in both cases, their appearance is altered by the differences in colour and surface texture of the papers.

HEALTH AND SAFETY

Always wear a mask when adding bronze, metal or lustre powders to a binder.

METALLIC BINDERS & MEDIA

Suitable binders for use on paper are acrylic varnishes, acrylic wax, metallic fabric medium (Ormaline), metallic paint medium, and acrylic texture gels. These binders will alter the surface finish of the powders. Gloss acrylic varnish emphasizes the sheen, whereas matt varnish will give a matt finish to the paper. Acrylic wax gives the paper a soft satin waxy finish with a more subtle, muted appearance. Ormaline metallic fabric medium is designed for applying powders to material, but it can also be used on paper; it has a slightly latex feel and is less runny when applied. Texture gels, as mentioned previously, introduce another dimension and can be used not only to apply a thick layer of colour but also to leave either a rough or smooth texture.

MIXING THE POWDERS INTO A BINDER

- Bronze and lustre powders are best mixed when you require them, and it is advisable to mix only small quantities at a time. The metal powders will tend to deteriorate with exposure to moisture and air. If a mixture is left, the powders will in some cases react with the binders, making them thicker and more awkward to apply.
- Select the binder that is suitable for the finish and technique you require.
- Most binders require about a tablespoon (15 ml) of binder to a teaspoon (5 ml) of bronze or lustre powder. You may need to add more bronze powders to the texture gels, depending on their finish.

▶ Lilac lustre powder, light gold metallic powder and green/gold Pearl Ex lustre powder were mixed with acrylic varnish. Using a broad paint brush, the coloured varnish was painted in stripes on pressed banana paper and worked into the surface of laid lokta paper, mixing the different iridescent colours together.

▶▶ Red Indian cotton rag paper. rubbed with red, purple and copper iridescent Paintstik.

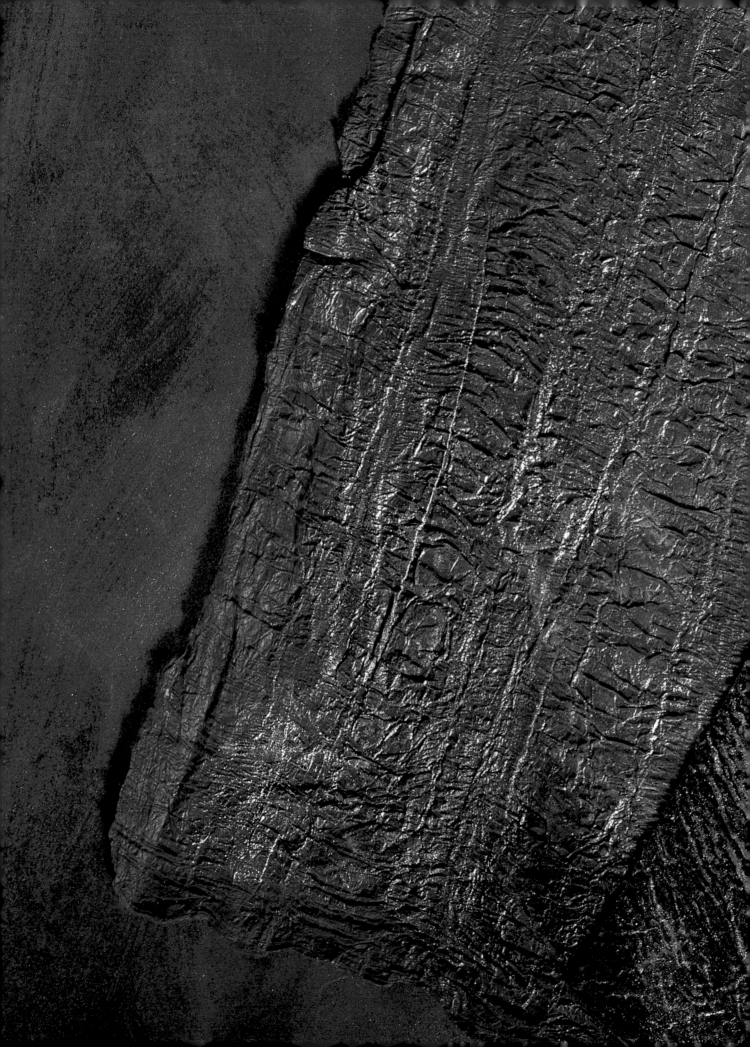

(Preceding page, from left to right) Black paper with green, blue, mauve lustre powder mixed with metallic powder medium and applied with a brush; dark blue ruched paper brushed wirh numerous bronze and lustre powders; black textured handmade paper brushed with middle gold metallic powder, lilac lustre powder and green gold Pearl Ex powder mixed with gloss acrylic varnish; greaseproof paper varnished with gold and copper iridescent acrylic and gloss varnish.

- To obtain a slight sheen, add only a small amount of powder; if a really dense metal surface is needed, add more powder.
- Remember, the greater the quantity of bronze powder added to the binder, the stiffer it will become. The powder therefore changes the nature of the binder.
- On contact with the binder, the bronze powder will change colour and lose its sheen, because it has become moist. The sheen will reappear once mixture has been applied and left to dry on the paper.
- The final effect of a lustre powder will be difficult to evaluate when it is first mixed with the binder, but its full potential will be revealed once it has been applied to paper and left to dry.
- The mixed medium will need to be slightly thinner if it is to be applied with a brush than it would if it were being used for printing.

ACRYLIC IRIDESCENT, METALLIC AND INTERFERENCE COLOURS

When confronted with the extensive range of acrylic iridescent, metallic and interference colours available in many art shops, it can be difficult to know what they will look like and how they will perform.

These colours are made with mica flakes held in an acrylic suspension. The mica flakes are very visible in iridescent or pearlescent tinting medium, especially when used on the darker papers. Metallic acrylics are iridescent colours, and provide rich, shimmering, reflective colours, including gold, silver, copper, bronze and stainless steel. The colours are conveniently available in tube and jar form, both of which are excellent for colouring papers.

Interference colours are created by giving a fine layer of titanium coating to the mica. This causes the light to bounce through the layers of acrylic, reflecting off the mica flakes as the paper is moved. An interference colour may be mixed with an opposite colour, to create a contrast, or applied directly, to give a coloured pearl finish. The colours are most easily seen when used on a darker ground, although more delicate effects can be achieved on lighter papers.

IRIDESCENT PAINTSTIKS

Iridescent Paintstik colours (see page 22) are mixed with a pearl binder. The resulting range of colours can be used on dark papers to create a lustrous surface. The colour is soft and can be rubbed, smeared or brushed on any porous surface. It can be used to enhance textured paper surfaces or to make rubbings through lightweight papers, or it can be worked into heavier papers or textured surfaces, like a polish. The range includes blue, greens, turquoise, purple, red, pink, orange and light gold, as well as copper, brown, charcoal, white, gold and silver. The colours will easily blend together, and iridescent blending sticks will extend the colour and make lighter pearl colours. By mixing a Professional Paintstik colour, such as grape, with an iridescent blending stick, you can create further iridescent colours.

Remember that a Paintstik can be used on its own, applied to dry acrylic colour, or used as a resist with dyes and inks (see also page 41).

MATERIALS
- selection of papers with surface textures, or a dark smooth paper
- Iridescent Paintstiks and iridescent blending stick

METHOD
1 Select any textured paper and apply some iridescent colour by rubbing the Paintstik directly on the paper.
2 Work a second colour into the paper and mix together. Rub the applied colour across the paper; you can do this with your finger, or directly from the stick, or even with an old toothbrush.
3 Depending on the surface of the paper, the Paintstik should move fairly easily, filling any crevices and highlighting any raised areas of paper.
4 Paintstiks can also be used to add emphasis to previously painted, inked or printed papers – just rub or brush areas to give extra colour or lustre as required.

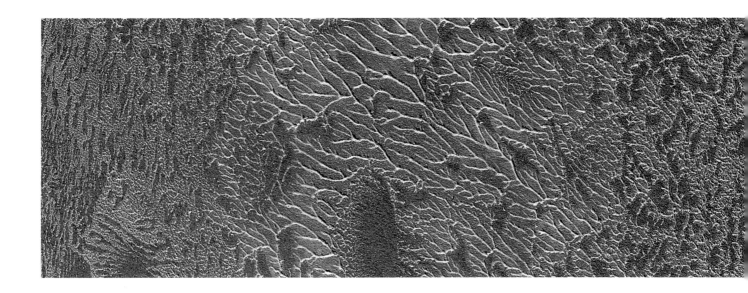

PAINTING METALLIC PAPERS

Mixed with an appropriate binder, metallic and lustre powders can be used to create stunning – and truly glorious – metallic papers.

MATERIALS

*   preferably darker-coloured papers, including brown paper, pre-inked greaseproof, cotton rag papers, such as rough banana or bagasse (made with sugar-cane fibre), ruched paper, or the heavier lokta papers and some of the stronger Japanese papers
*   bronze or lustre powders
*   acrylic varnish or acrylic wax
*   mask
*   small jars for mixing powders
*   palette knife
*   paint brushes (synthetic or fine bristle brushes) and small pieces of sponge

METHOD

1   Mix a selection of bronze or lustre powders in acrylic varnish, gloss or matt, or acrylic wax. Three different colours will be sufficient to start with, as further combinations will appear as they intermingle.

2   Select the papers you wish to use, choosing a range offering different colours and surfaces. You might pick a smooth light paper, a thicker utilitarian paper and maybe a more extravagant handmade textured paper.

3   Gently brush the metallic colour into the surface of the paper. Work it in several directions, as the powders will glisten in different ways, depending on the angle at which they catch the light.

4   Apply some of a bronze or lustre powder mix with broad smooth brush strokes, so that it fully covers areas of the paper. Next, apply the colour lightly, using a brush that is almost dry and barely touching the surface of the paper. This will give fine lines of colour, differing from one paper to another.

5   Repeat the same processes with each of your bronze and lustre colours until you have achieved an effect that pleases you.

6   Always allow the paper to dry between applications in order to see the finished effect of the colour and to prevent colours merging.

7   Each paper will absorb the acrylic varnish or wax in a different way: the greaseproof will probably crinkle up, whereas the textural surface of the Asian papers will be enhanced by the richness of the metallic and lustre finishes.

▲ Interference gold, green, purple, blue and red acrylic were used to make this glass-plate organic print on Canson paper.

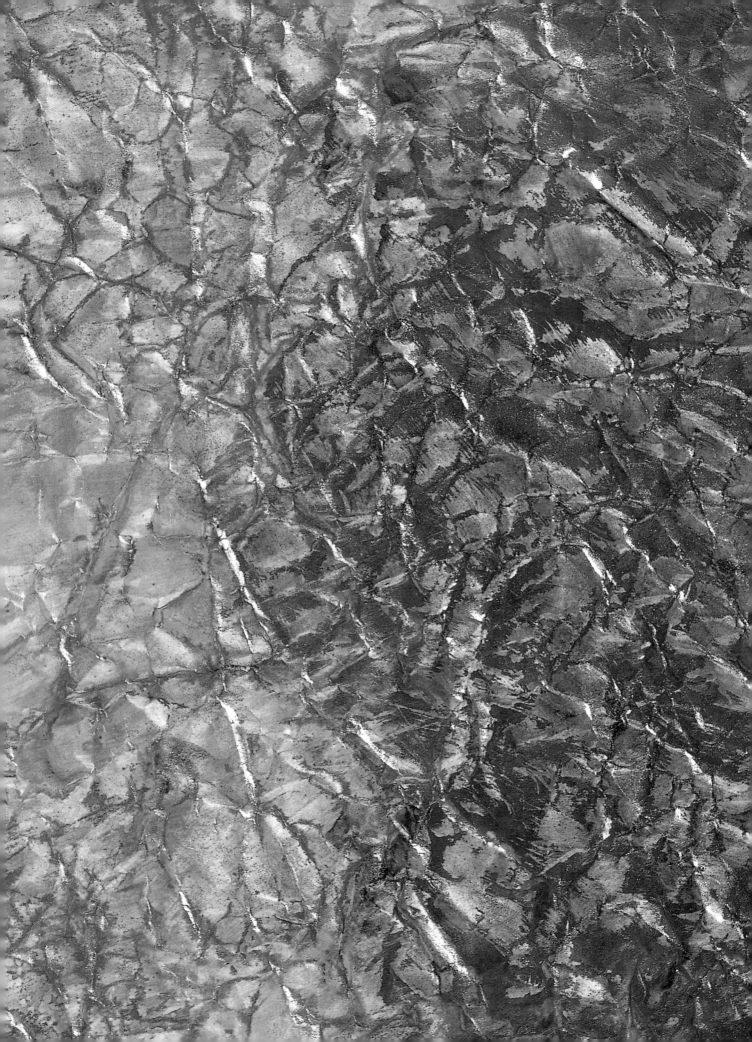

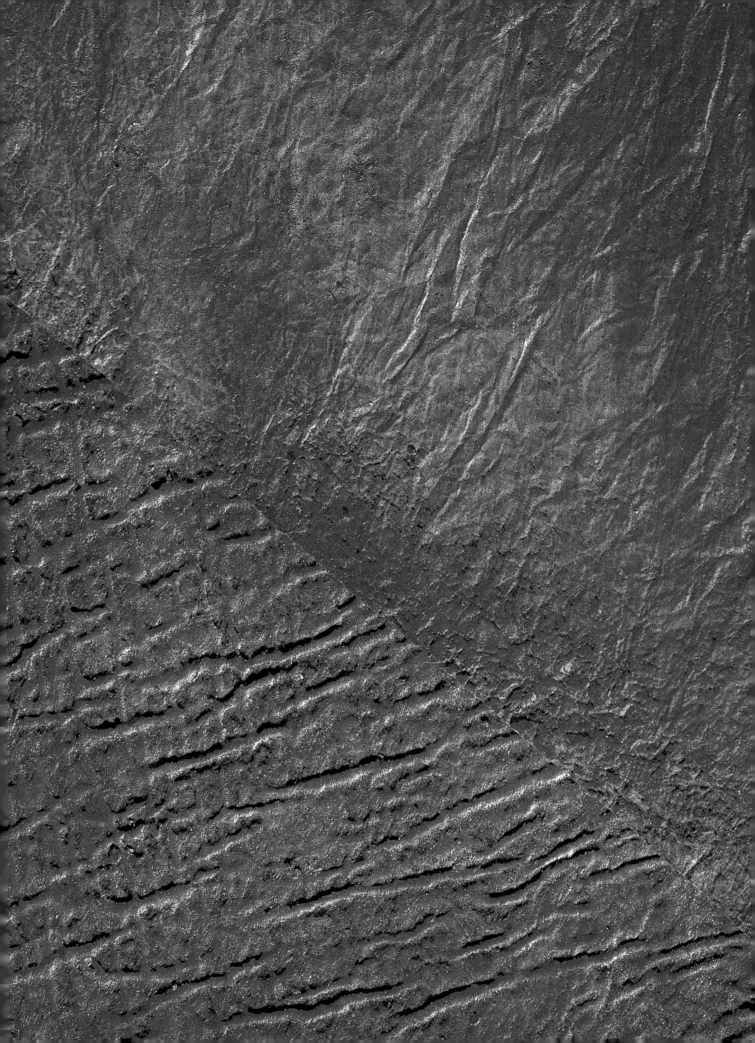

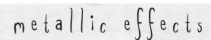

CRUMPLED METALLIC SURFACES

1 Use a medium-to-fine weight of paper – one that will withstand being crumpled.
2 Screw the paper up several times, until the surface is covered with fine cracks. Flatten the paper slightly, and lightly brush different bronze and lustre powders across the distressed surface of the paper.
3 Allow the paper to dry and repeat the process until the paper has a facetted appearance.
4 Once dry, the paper can be further enhanced with inks or dye.
5 Some handmade papers have very textured or creased surfaces which can be emphasized by gentle brushing with bronze and lustre powders, to show up the character of the paper.
6 Remember that the addition of acrylic wax or varnishes will serve to strengthen these papers, as well as changing the handling quality of the surface.

PRINTED METALLIC PAPERS

A number of metallic papers can be created with the printing techniques already described (see pages 56–62). Metallic, interference and iridescent acrylics are all suitable for use with these techniques, as are bronze and lustre powders, mixed with the various metallic binders.

MATERIALS

- smooth paper, such as coloured cartridge, black paper or lightweight card
- acrylic metallic, iridescent and interference colours, or bronze and lustre powders, mixed with Ormaline or heavy gel media
- round-bladed knife or palette knife
- two sheets of laminated plastic or toughened glass

(Preceding page) White Conqueror paper was repeatedly crumpled and iridescent lustre powders and acrylic wax were applied. Some areas have two or more layers of lustre powder, giving subtle changes of iridescent colour. Once the acrylic wax was dry, the paper was inked with ultramarine dye.

◀ Iridescent blue, purple and white Paintstiks were worked into heavy silk paper and rubbed onto textured black paper.

(Overleaf) Silver, gold, light gold, copper, brown and red iridescent Painstiks were applied with the iridescent blending stick in broad diagonal sweeps. The mica flakes will show on the surface of the colour, because of the direction in which they have been applied.

▶ Soft silk paper, light lokta and crinkle paper were all painted with dyes. Once dry, they were torn and glued together and then carefully and lightly brushed with bronze and lustre powders mixed with acrylic wax to emphasize the paper qualities.

METALLIC ORGANIC PRINT – METHOD

1 On one plastic sheet or glass plate, put small blobs either of any metallic, iridescent or interference acrylic colour, or of bronze or lustre powders, mixed with your chosen medium.

2 Place the second sheet on top of the first and gently squeeze the two together.

3 Rotate the two sheets a little to make sure that the colours have mixed slightly and the plates are fully covered.

4 Carefully prise the plates apart with a round-bladed knife; there should now be a fernlike pattern across both surfaces.

5 Lay the plates on a flat surface and carefully place a sheet of paper on the raised colour of one sheet. Gently press the paper on the colour to release the pattern from the printing surface.

6 The effect should be very rich, with the different metallic and iridescent colours mixing in varying densities and colour combinations (see photograph on page 83).

7 Further prints may be achieved, but remember each print will reduce the amount of colour left, so use a finer and lighter paper to lift the remaining colour off the print surface.

8 This technique is particularly effective if a series of interference colours is used, as these will mix and reflect the light in different ways, depending on the angle at which the paper is held.

9 Do not press the heavy gel medium too hard, as the aim is to retain the raised peaked surface.

BLOCK-AND-ROLLER PRINTS

Metallic and lustre powders, mixed into either Ormaline binder or one of the smooth texture gels, will also make very good block-and-roller prints. Use the techniques described on pages 58–62.

SPREADING ACRYLIC INTERFERENCE COLOURS

Select a series of iridescent and interference acrylic colours. Use a palette knife to spread them on a sheet of smooth or lightly textured paper.

Sweep the knife across so that the interference and iridescent colours are mixed. When spread with a knife in this way, the colours will mix with varying degrees of intensity.

LAYERING LUSTRE AND METALLIC PAPERS

Once you have used pearl, iridescent, bronzed and metallic media to make a number of papers, you can combine these to create other, complex and unique papers.

Make a selection of papers that have been previously coloured. It is helpful if they are similar in weight; for example, you might select a range comprising tissue, greaseproof paper, light lokta paper and crinkle paper.

Tear or cut the different papers into strips, and arrange the strips, slightly overlapping them. You might perhaps add a few plain papers. Coat the finished design with either acrylic wax or acrylic varnish to create a new sheet of paper. The varnish or wax can either be used uncoloured, or – to give an overall unity – dye or even bronze or lustre powders may be added.

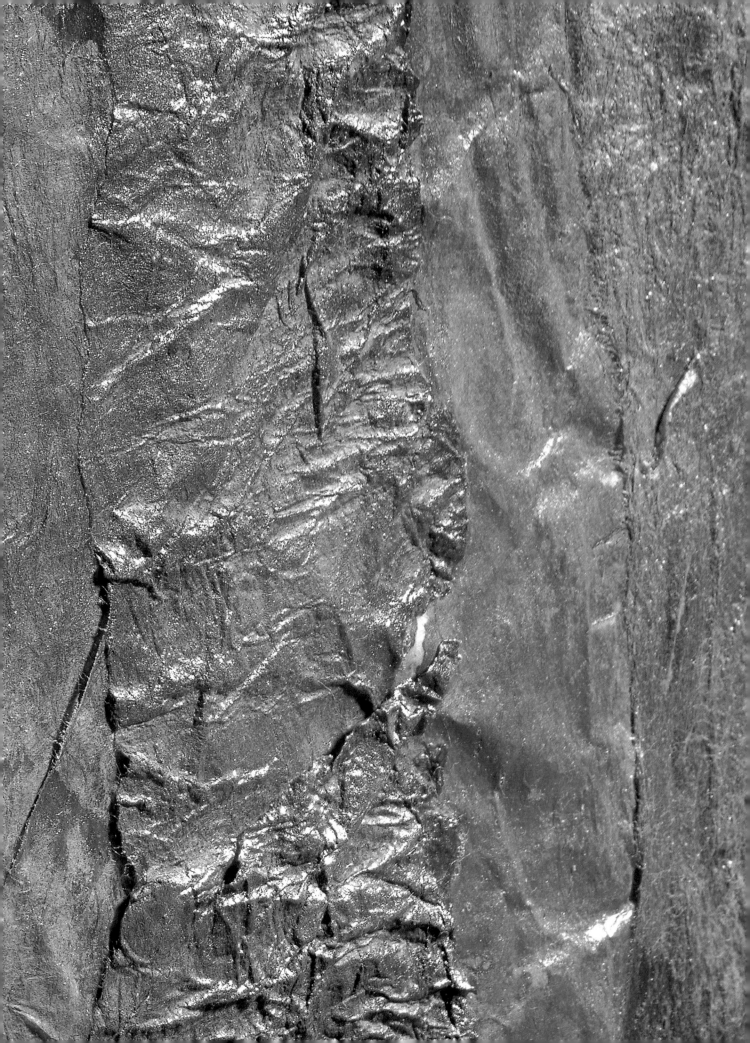

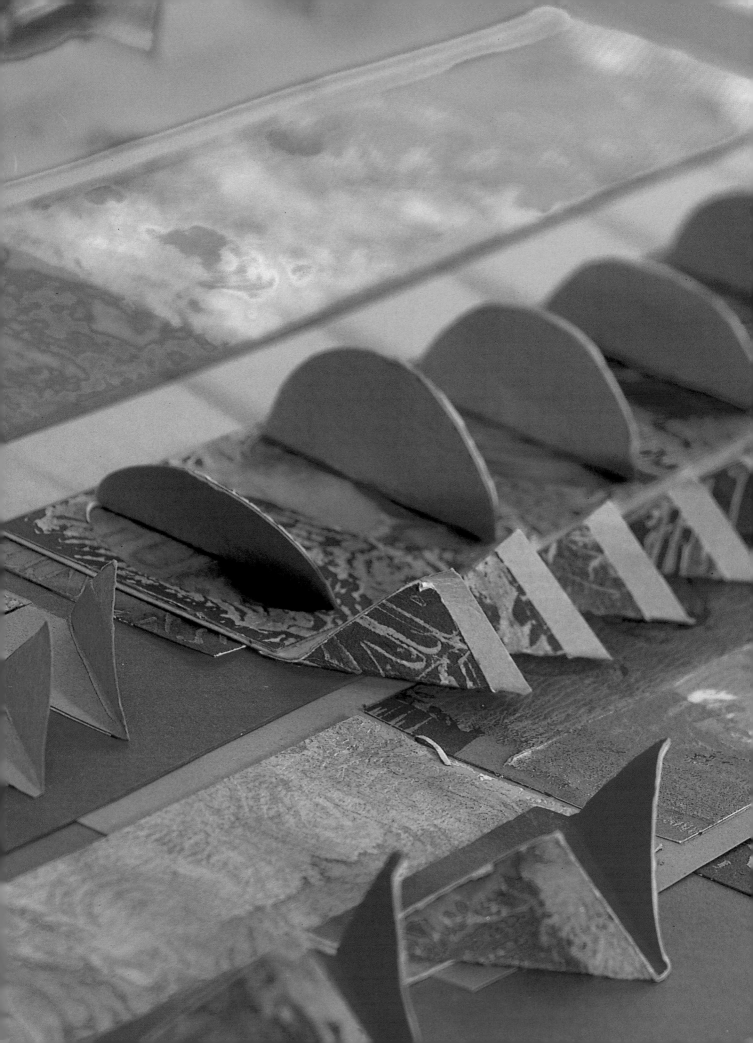

eight
Designing with Papers

There are so many ways of putting together colour, pattern, shape, texture

and line into compositions, it is difficult to know where to start. Artists and

designers have always written, discussed and argued about the composition of

work, so it is unlikely that a right or wrong way can be established in a short

chapter! However, there are some tips that might prove helpful for those who

are less experienced or who lack confidence. Do not think of them as rules,

more as suggestions that might help.

Illustration: A series of printed papers were glued onto contrasting plain papers, and sometimes a further piece of printed paper was glued to the back of the paper. Some strips were cut with a craft knife — mainly straight cuts so that it was possible to open windows in the strips and view other papers or colour through the aperture created. The strips were positioned, further colours being selected to frame, emphasize, or combine areas together. There is a freedom working with paper compositions, because it is possible to position different elements and then adjust the effect by adding or removing papers.

DESIGN TIPS

- Firstly, try to study other things that are designed or composed.
- Study the layout of a newspaper page – analyse where the most important area is in a two-page spread. Is it the top right-hand corner or the bottom left; where do they put the juiciest picture or the dullest advert?
- What makes you linger on the page and not turn over, and are there spaces and gaps between text and photographs?
- Study a painting that you like. Why does it attract you? Is it the colour, texture, style or subject matter? Is there a particular area that is the focal point, and if so where is it? Does the picture have different areas that give it depth, and are there hidden areas? Some pictures may be very complex; others may be quite simple, but just as effective.
- Think about arranging objects on a mantelpiece or a window ledge; you might even try it, if you like. Would you arrange them in a symmetrical fashion – clock in the middle, candle at either end, with perhaps a pair of vases in between? Would you place the clock at one end and group the candlesticks together towards the right, perhaps with the vases in between? Everyone will have different preferences, but some arrangements are more pleasing than others. How you use an arrangement depends on how you want to express your design ideas.
- Having a slightly wider frame, border or piece at the bottom of a composition will give it weight and make the design feel stable. Putting the weightier pieces at the top of the composition, on the other hand, will make the design both less stable and less static.
- Compositions can become over-crowded and congested with colour, pattern, texture and shapes. If you remove some of the elements, a design may become livelier, and you can give greater emphasis to areas that you want to highlight.
- Plain papers can give a sense of space, with areas of calm.

Here are some further ideas for composing a design:

- To give a sense of flow in a design, so that the eye is led naturally from one area to another, it helps if you create the impression of a line in the desired direction. This may be solid or dotted, or can even be formed by the edges of various shapes. The eye will jump gaps in a line, so do not feel that it has to be continuous.
- Lines can be used tie up parts of the design into little self-contained packages or sections.
- A line that is intersected by other lines will interrupt the rhythm. This can be used to be disruptive or can give a sense of juddering, jumpy movement.
- Undulating, curving lines will give the feeling of gentle movement, like waves, whereas zigzags will give sharp pointed effects.
- Allow the design to lie in the middle of the background, leaving space around it, almost like a frame.

SELECTING PAPERS AND COLOURS

When using your coloured papers to create designs, you will need to choose some plain coloured papers to complement them. Excellent ranges of commercially produced coloured papers are available through the larger art shops. These are now often available in A4 sheets or in pads. Many people consider that a pack of cheap sugar paper will be adequate, but the limited colours and dull paper surface will do little to complement your papers.

Accumulate a stock of coloured papers from which to select when the need arises. Make sure your store includes tints and shades and colours from the entire spectrum. If you are unable to purchase a sufficiently varied collection, mix a range of dyes or acrylics and spend some time painting your own range of plain coloured papers.

▶ Two sheets of printed paper were selected – one roller printed, one block printed. Both papers were cut into equal strips and kept in order. The strips were then laid out; spaces were left between each strip, and the second print was laid at right angles to the first. The resulting grid was glued together and laid on various coloured grounds. Finally, the red background was selected as this enriched the colour and emphasized the texture and pattern of the printing.

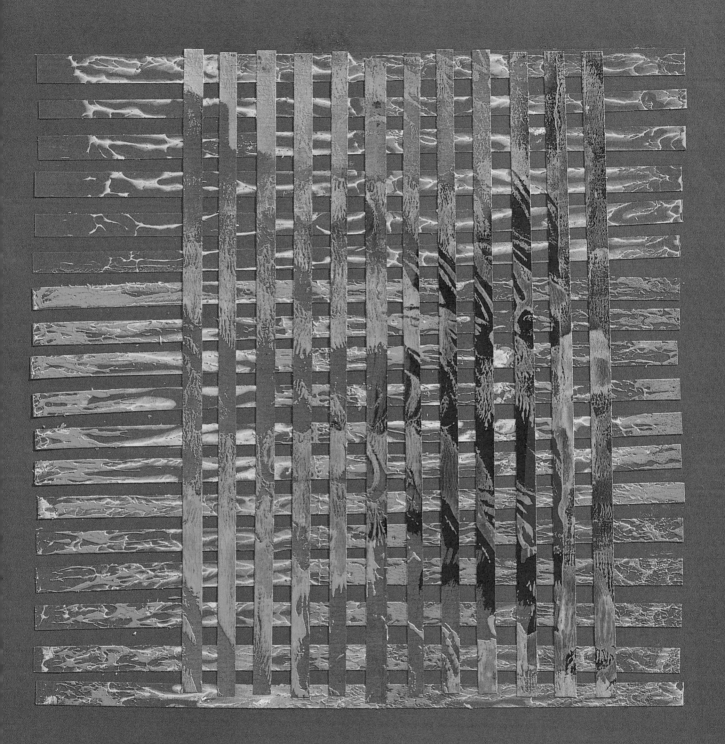

ORGANIZING YOUR COLLECTION

By now you will have gathered together a varied collection of glorious decorated papers. There will be flat colour, mottled textures and patterned surfaces, as well as varnishes and resists. There will be metallic surfaces and shimmering lustre finishes, and some pieces incorporating a number of techniques.

Collect all these papers together and add some plain coloured papers. Spend time sorting out your collection: take a good look at the papers, lay them out on the table, and observe them from different directions and in different lights. Try to get to know them. You might sort them into colours – reds, blues and yellows together – or textures, or techniques. You could put patterns together, or the metallic surfaces, or glossy finishes.

It is often helpful, and fun, to document small areas of each paper into a small spiral-bound sketchbook, making brief notes about each paper, including the techniques and materials used. The book will be your own unique diary, a really useful reference document, and you will feel very worthy because you have filed all this information!

When sorting, you will be looking at the papers and analysing them. Try to decide why you like one piece better than another. Would some of the pieces look better if they had another coat of ink or if more printing were applied?

It is worth trying out some of these ideas to see what happens. Select a piece that you feel is not 'working'; add more colour, and see how it changes. Somehow it feels less dangerous working on an unsatisfactory piece than on one you love.

Some papers you will never want to cut up, while others may seem a mess and you might even want to put them in the bin. Before you go to that extreme, stop and try some of the following ideas.

ISOLATING AND FRAMING

A large area of randomly painted, printed and coloured paper can be overwhelming. Too many patterns, colours and elements can seem to fight for your attention. There are a number of ways to overcome this.

- Select areas by cutting the paper into regular shapes, such as squares, strips and blocks.
- Isolate areas in order to look at limited parts of the paper and then select specific sections you might want to use.
- Divide the paper up by adding pieces of plain paper, either inserted or attached to the first piece.
- If the paper is really too precious to be cut up, get a colour photocopy or a scanned print and cut this up instead.

CUT STRIPS

For a basic arrangement of strips, select a piece of patterned paper, perhaps about A4 in size, and carefully divide it into parallel strips, either of equal widths or a variety of widths. Keeping the cut strips in the order in which you cut them, separate them with pieces of plain coloured paper, chosen to enhance the patterned surface of the original paper.

FURTHER EFFECTS
- Lay the strips in a straight vertical or horizontal arrangement to create weaves, meshes and grids.
- Step the strips up and down to create waves.
- Lay the strips diagonally.
- Vary the width of the spaces between the patterned strips by using differing widths of plain coloured paper.

TEARING SKILLS

Apart from cutting your papers, you can tear them to create a variety of effects. The paper that you select will dictate the nature of torn edge: some will be difficult to tear, some too thick, and some too fine, but others will give soft, almost fringed edges. There will be a contrast in sheen, texture and colour between the torn edge of a coloured paper that has been printed and the printed surface. The applied media will affect the tear: acrylics and

▶ Strips of equal size were cut from two areas of the same sheet of paper – one area printed and inked, the other just inked – and were laid on a contrasting paper in an alternating pattern. The strips were kept in the correct order and the inked half was stepped up and down to form a curve.

varnishes will strengthen the paper and give firmer stronger edges, while dyes and repeated crumpling can soften and weaken paper, giving a softer edge.

Before rushing headlong into tearing up all your decorated papers, spend a short while considering and practising your tearing technique! The following points should all be borne in mind.

- Paper has a grain, and a horizontal tear will look different to vertical one.
- Realise that you work with a left- or right-hand bias, and that the angle at which you hold the paper will alter the width of the torn edge.
- If you want a torn edge that is shallow but straight, tear the paper against a ruler.
- If you tear a curve or circle from the printed side of the paper, the tear will remain close to the surface

colour. Tear from the reverse, and there will be an edge of torn plain paper around the printed area.

- Machine-made industrial and commercial papers, such as printer paper, cartridge and brown paper, will tend to tear fairly evenly and easily.
- Fine Asian papers, such as lokta, ruched paper and Indian cotton rag papers, will tend to tear less evenly, and the edge will reveal fibres of different lengths.
- Fine papers, such as mulberry tissue, silk papers or straw silk papers, are also difficult to control, as they tend to rip, but sometimes they give a very soft fluffy edge, often with long fibres.
- It may help you to control the tear if you gently dampen the paper where you wish to tear it.
- Finally, be aware of the individual deckle edges that are part of all the handmade papers and use these to best advantage.

◀◀ A printed paper was cut into strips of different lengths. The strips were then woven with strips of varying widths cut from plain papers. The woven paper was glued to a backing paper to hold it in position. This sheet was then cut into strips, diagonally across the weave, and these were spaced out and mounted on a sympathetic background.

◀ An area of inked paper was carefully torn to make best use of the quality and colour of the torn edge. This was glued to a page of an Indian cotton rag sketchbook.

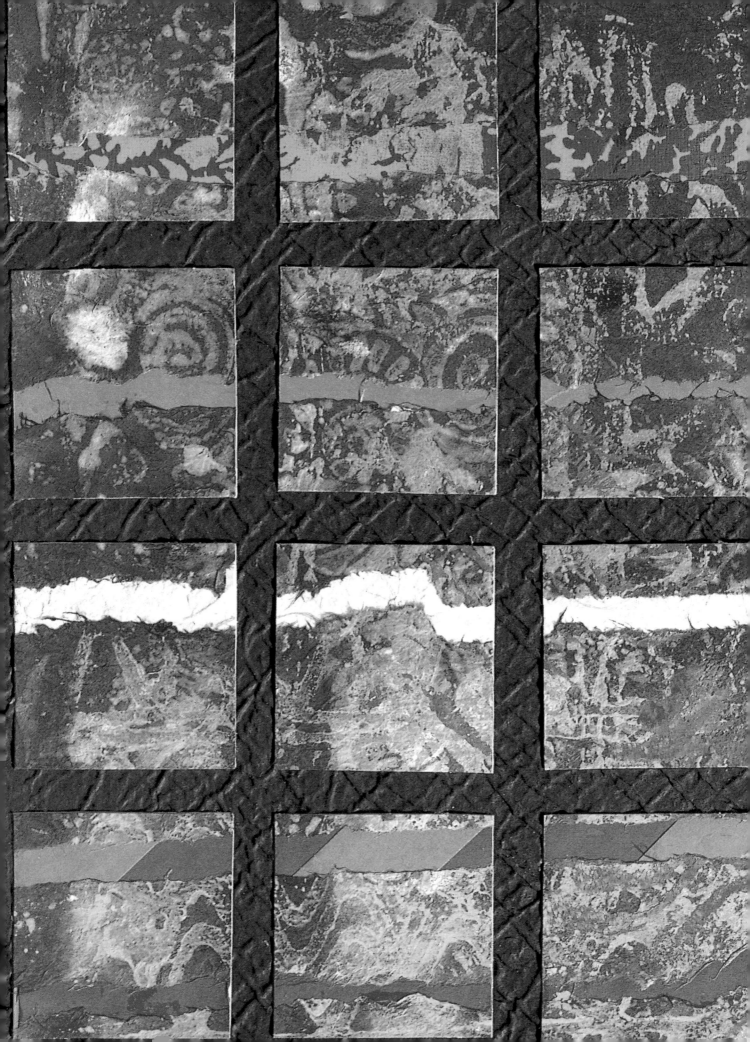

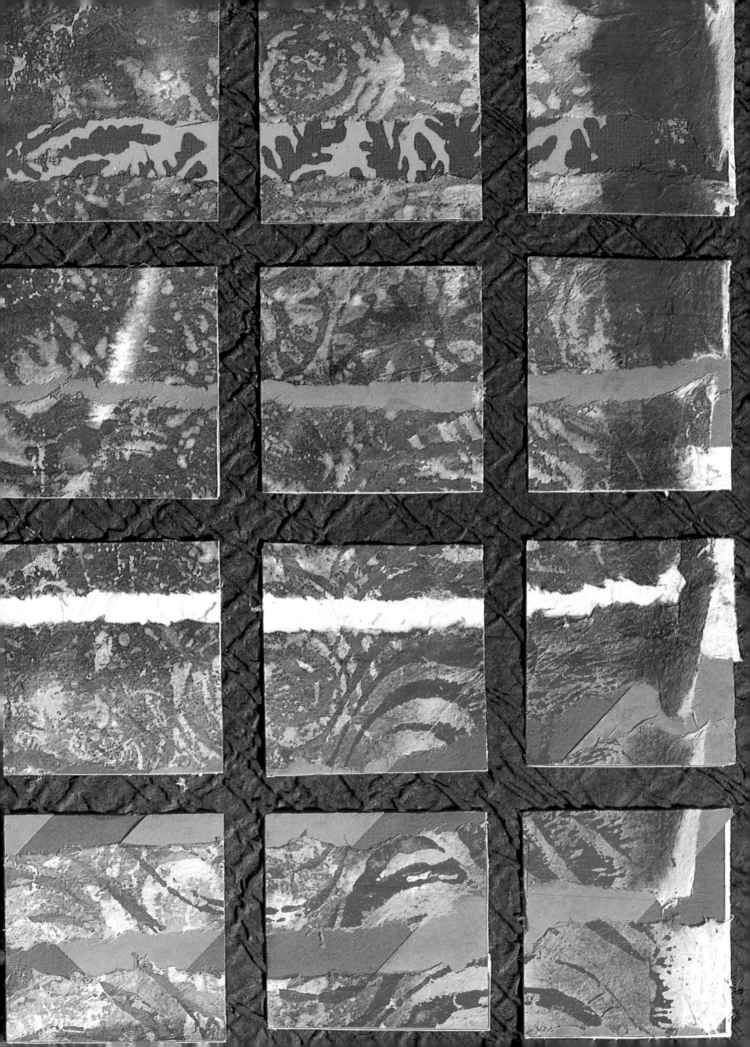

(Preceding page)
Cut and torn edges are used extensively by gluing torn sections of a printed paper onto contrasting papers, either plain or patterned. This reorganized piece of paper was then cut into equal squares and placed onto a textured black paper. By dividing this piece into squares, attention is drawn to separate areas rather than being overwhelmed by the whole piece.

◀ Using right-angled templates, an area of the print was isolated, cut out and applied to a plain paper, and then framed with another patterned printed paper. Finally, it was mounted on a sympathetic background paper.

> ▶ A light card template was cut using bead shapes, ovals, and strung together. This template was used to frame areas of selected papers that were then cut out. The papers were then arranged, with other areas of the papers that complimented the composition. Different surface finishes and paper types are more noticeable when placed next to each other and finally set on a background colour.

LAYERING TORN PAPERS

If you take care to select different weights, textures and types of paper, you can create further sheets of paper by layering torn strips or areas of papers together. These sheets of paper can be made of uncoloured natural papers, such as different weights of lokta, straw silk, and ruched paper, so that the surfaces and textures are emphasized.

Layers of torn coloured papers create a very useful subtle texture when combined with printed and dyed papers. For support, the layers can all be glued to a lightweight background paper.

You might like to explore some of the following suggestions.

- Take a sheet of patterned or dyed paper and carefully tear it into strips. You might tear at a slightly diagonal angle. Rearrange these strips on a plain piece of paper in a contrast colour, maybe overlapping the strips or spacing them out to create a pleasing arrangement.
- Tear and cut strips of printed and plain coloured paper, and then rearrange them into stripped patterns or simple grids or weaves. The contrasts between the soft torn edges and the hard cut ones will add variety to the design.
- Create a paper that is composed of a torn printed, plain and textured paper. This can create a complicated and complex image. Carefully cut this paper into regular strips or squares and reposition on a sympathetic background. The careful regular cutting will emphasize the areas of complex irregular pattern by framing them, and this also offers an opportunity to add space and colour to the composition.

TWO RIGHT-ANGLED TEMPLATES

The following is a useful way of deciding which areas of a paper to select for a design.

MATERIALS

- paper(s) for design
- card
- scalpel or craft knife
- metal ruler
- cutting board

METHOD

1 Using the scalpel or knife and metal rule, make yourself two L-shaped pieces of light card. These can be placed together to make a frame which can then be adjusted to enclose different areas of your paper – squares, rectangles, wedges, or narrow strips.

2 As you experiment with your adjustable frame, you will discover more areas of your paper that you like. You might try making a particular rectangle larger or smaller, to see how the decoration and colour alters.

3 Next, you might cut some of these squares, rectangles or other shapes from the sheet of paper to isolate them. Use a small craft knife, a safety metal ruler and a cutting board rather than a pair of scissors. The paper will stay flat when it is cut with a craft knife, and you can easily see where and what you are cutting. Cutting with scissors often damages the paper and is less accurate.

4 Remember to check the paper that has had the shape cut from it; this can often make an attractive frame for later use.

SHAPED TEMPLATES

(Preceding page) A number of different circular and oval templates were drawn and cut out. A range of different papers was selected, inked, varnished, textured and printed, but all within a bright blue/green purple colour scheme. A few additional papers were required to give vibrancy and variety, including a touch of yellow and orange. Areas of the papers were cut out with a sharp craft knife, and the pieces were then arranged until the composition was complete. The result was then placed on a piece of natural lokta walnut paper, which seemed to bring out the richness of the colours and the differing surfaces.

The logical progression from simple right-angled frames is to make a more complex template or stencil.

- Make a shaped frame so that designs can be created using multiple images taken from a range of coloured and patterned papers.
- Moving the template across the paper, identify attractive areas; cut them out, and gradually build up a pile of shaped papers ready to use. This is like selecting colours, textures and patterns for a patchwork or samples for decorating a room.
- Be aware, as you cut out, of the negative areas of paper, the areas cut around the image, which could also be used in your design.
- Cut out some further plain coloured shapes to complement the painted and patterned pieces.

USING THE CUT SHAPES

- Take a large sheet of paper, probably bigger than you ultimately want your design to be, and start to place your cut pieces on it.
- Be aware of the spaces between the shapes; notice how they relate to and complement each other without detracting from each other.
- Watch the space between the shapes; do not allow this to become too great or the design may appear rather dismembered.
- Try to build up areas of interest with a few shapes very close together, almost grouping. Some shapes might even be overlapped, which will alter their

relationship, and this might perhaps be countered with an area of plain coloured paper.
- Move the pieces around on the sheet of paper, experimenting with different colours of paper beside, behind and on top of the patterned pieces.
- Try several background colours until you find an arrangement that is pleasing.
- Some arrangements will appeal to you, while you will find others less attractive, but only you can decide which arrangement is best and why.
- To check whether you feel that the arrangement is working well, temporarily hold the pieces in place by lightly attaching them to the background with small pieces of masking tape.
- Pin your arrangement to a vertical surface and step back to view it.
- It is often worth leaving the piece for a while. After this, you can come back and view it again with a fresh eye.

CONCLUSION

Having made a pile of glorious papers, keep them readily available in a folder or a drawer, so that they can be used for all kinds of projects or events. Note the techniques in your sketchbook, so that you have a record of your artistic journey.

Little isolated rectangles can either be used to make personal cards, or pieced together to cover books, portfolios and boxes. Combined with further drawing and painting, these coloured papers can be the basis for a multitude of designs, plans and pictures.

Hopefully, the papers and techniques described in this book will only be the beginning of an exciting voyage of experiment and discovery.

glorious papers

LIST OF SUPPLIERS

UK

Arjo Wiggins Fine Papers Ltd
Cateway House
PO Box 88
Lime Tree Way
Chineham
Basingstoke
Hants RG24 8BA
Tel: 0800 993300
Fax: 01322 335620
www.conqueror.com

Wide variety of commercial papers, including metallic and interference papers in various weights as well as fine smooth papers, such as Conqueror.

Art Van Go
16 Hollybush Lane
Datchworth
Knebworth
Herts SG3 6RE
Tel: 01438 814946
Fax: 01438 816267
Email: *artvango@talk21.com*

Mail order with informative catalogue and a mobile art van supplying an extensive range of handmade papers, acrylic colour, wax and varnish as well as bronze/lustre powders and Markal Paintstiks, pump spray etc; will supply worldwide.

Colourcraft
Unit 5
555 Carlisle Street East
Sheffield S4 8DT
Tel/Fax: 0114 242 1431

Dytek dyes, Brusho inks and lustre powders, useful literature; will supply worldwide.

Daler Rowney Ltd
PO Box 10
Bracknell
Berkshire RG12 8ST
Tel: 01344 424621
Fax: 01344 486511

Artist's materials – acrylics, including interference colours, texture pastes, Canford paper, glaze media and product literature.

Golden Artists Colours
Global Art Supplies Ltd
Unit 8
Leeds Place
Tollington Park
London N4 3QW
Tel: 0207 281 2451
Fax: 0207 281 7693
Email: mail@gas.demon.co.uk

Artist's materials – wide range of texture gels, acrylic iridescent colour and interference colours and literature about the media.

Levermore & Co Ltd
24 Endeavour Way
London SW19 8UH
Tel: 0208 946 9882
(Markal Paintstiks.)

Liquitex Acrylics
COLART Craft Network
Whitefriars Avenue
Harrow
Middlesex HA3 5RH
Tel: 0208 427 4343

Liquitex acrylic colours and range of texture gels plus literature, and Winsor and Newton products.

Mulberry Papers
2 Old Rectory Cottages
Easton Grey
Malmesbury
Wiltshire SN16 0PE
Tel/Fax: 01666 841028
   Collection of exotic and handmade papers from Thailand by mail order; UK only.

Procion Dyes – Jacquard
Email: *kim@jacquardproducts.com* for local store listing

C. Roberson & Co Ltd
1A Hercules Street
London N7 6AT
Tel: 020 7272 0567
Fax: 020 7263 0212
   Bronze powders – full range of metallic powders – UK only unless wholesale.

USA

Arjo Wiggins Fine Papers Ltd
Mike Carlisle
Tel: 001920 830 4010
Fax: 001920 830 4016
Email: *michael@curiouspapers.com*

Daler Rowney USA
3 Corporate Drive
Cranbury
NJ 0851-9584
Tel: 001609 655 5252
Fax: 001609 655 5825

Daniel Smith
4150 First Avenue South
PO Box 84268
Seattle
WA 98124-5568
Tel: 001206 223 9599
Toll free no: 800 2384065
www.danielsmith.com
   Papers and art materials.

Golden Artist Colour Inc
188 Bell Road
New Berlin
New York 13411–9527
Tel: 001607 847 6154
www.goldenpaints.com

Shiva (Markal Paintstiks)
Jack Richeson & Co
PO Box 160
Kimberly
Winsconsin 54136
Tel: 001920 738 0744
Toll free no: 800 2332404

Artist & Craftsman Supply
Tel: 001800 876 8076
www.artistcraftsman.com

COLART America Inc
11 Constitution Avenue
PO Box 1396
Piscataway
NJ 08855–1396
Tel: 001732 562 0770

AUSTRALIA

Arjo Wiggins Fine Papers Ltd
Will Boom
Tel: 00612 941 73888
Fax: 00612 941 73886
Email: *arjoaus@arjowiggins.com.au*

Liquitex Australia
Jasco Pty Ltd
118–122 Bowden Street
Meadowbank
NSW 2114

INDEX

Bold type denotes
major references

A

acrylic colours see acrylic paints
    iridescent, metallic and
interference 82, 90
acrylic paints 22, **54–62**
acrylic varnish 49–52
    wax 49–52

B

bamboo strip paper 12
banana paper 12
batik 39
blending sticks 47
block-and-roller prints 90
block printing see printing
bronze and lustre powders see
metallic bronze and lustre powders
brown paper 12, 18
brushes 24
Brusho inks 19

C

cartridge paper 12, 18
collecting papers, for design 96
colour and texture, combining 73
colouring media **19–22**
colours, mixing 19, **28**, 55, 58
cotton paper 12
cutting strips, for design 96

D

design tips 94

E

equipment **24**

F

foam core board 24
Foamtastic 24

G

Gampi paper 12
glass plates 24
glass-plate printing see printing
grouting tools 24

H

health and safety advice 24, 72, 76
Hispeed paper 12

I

Indian cotton rag paper 18
    Southern Indian 18
Indian ruched paper 12
Indian silk paper, 18
inks, adding to prints 62
    adding to texture gels 72

K

Keaycolour paper 12
kozo paper 12

L

layering papers 52
    lustre and metallic papers 90
    torn papers 104
lokta paper 12, 18
    lokta huck 12
    lokta wood dust 12

M

Markal Paintstiks see Paintstiks
materials **12–22**
metallic binders 78
metallic bronze and lustre powders
19, 51, 68, 76
    mixing 78, 82
mulberry tissue paper 12, 18

O

oil pastels 41
    iridescent 41

P

painting **32–36**
    crumpled papers 33, 87
    metallic papers 83
    sprayed papers 36
    stripes 32
Paintstiks 22, 41, 72–3
    iridescent 41, 82
palette 24, 28
papers **12–18**, 52
    coloured 94
    handmade 12, 18
    metallic 12
    textured 12
Pearl Ex 76
printing **56–62**
    block 58–62
    glass-plate, 58, 62
    metallic papers 87
    roller 58, 62
Procion dyes 19
pump spray 24, 36

R

resists 22, **41–52**
roller printing see printing

S

Sanwa paper 12
silk paper, 12
straw paper 12

T

tearing papers 96–104
templates, for design 104
    shaped templates 108
texture gels **66–73**, 78
    applying 72
    colouring 68
tissue paper 18

W

wax crayons 41
    candles 41

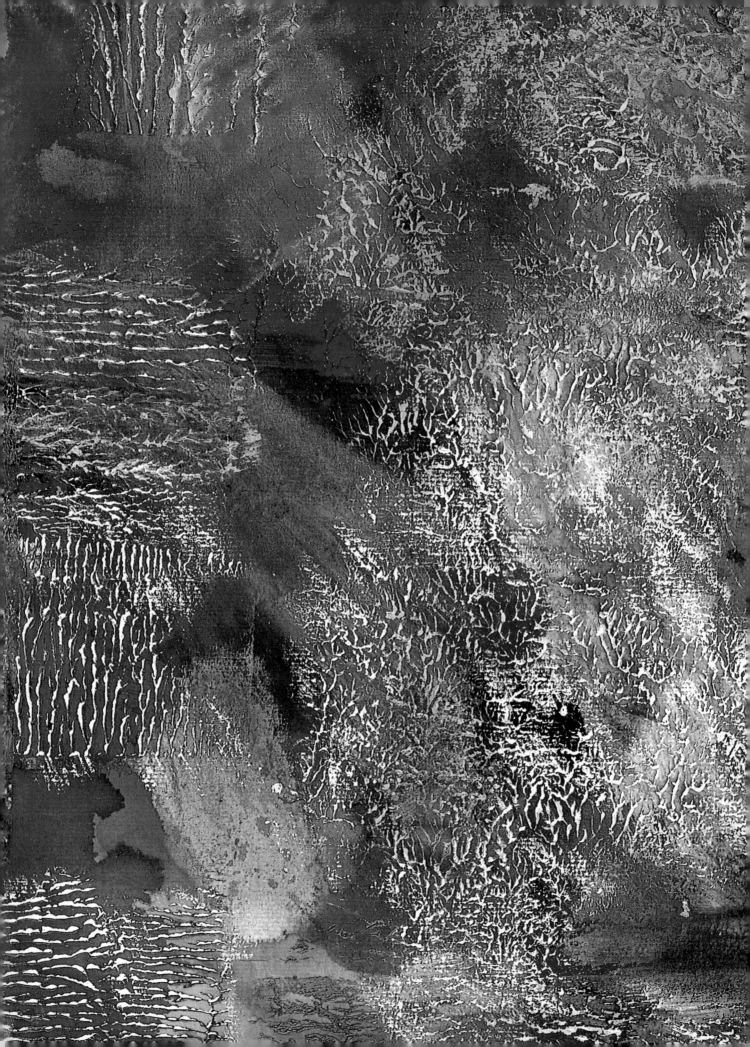